CW00553339

HORNBY magazine

What's inside...

6

Discover our Top 20 products of 2018.

Tim Shackleton shows how to weather and enhance Hornby Class 60s for 'OO' gauge.

Grosvenor Square has been extended and revitalised for a new lease of life in 2018.

EDITORIAL
Editor: Mike Wild
Assistant Editor: Mark Chivers
Sub Editor: Andy Roden
Group Editor - Transport: Roger Mortimer
Contributors: Evan Green-Hughes, Tim Shackleton, Trevor Jones, Tony Gee, Julia Scarlett and Ian Wild.
Senior designer: Steve Diggle

REGISTERED OFFICE
Units 1-4, Gwash Way Industrial Estate, Ryhall Road, Stamford, Lincs PE9 1XP

PRINTING
Gomer Press Limited, Llandysul Ceredigion, South Wales.

ADVERTISING
Advertising: Sarah Jarman
Email: sarah.jarman@keypublishing.com
Tel: 01780 755131 **Fax:** 01780 757261
Advertising Production: Rebecca Duffy
Tel: 01780 755131
Fax: 01780 757261
Email: rebecca.duffy@keypublishing.co.uk

PUBLISHING
Publisher: Adrian Cox
Tel: 01780 755131
Fax: 01780 757261
Email: adrian.cox@keypublishing.com

Group CEO: Adrian Cox
Commercial Director: Ann Saundry
Sales & Marketing Manager: Martin Steele

Key Publishing Ltd,
Units 1-4, Gwash Way Industrial Estate
Ryhall Road Stamford, Lincs PE9 1XP

Welc

NOSTALGIA takes on many forms and periods. In the past we've concentrated on the steam era for layout projects – a period which is full of nostalgia for those who experienced it first-hand and for modellers like myself who have marvelled with rose-tinted spectacles at the wonders of the steam age.

Sometimes it is difficult to remember just how fast things have changed and while the steam era is firmly at the heart of our modelling activities, we have been keen to explore new areas. We dabbled with the corporate blue era in Yearbook No. 8 when we built West Riding Power in 'N' gauge and we've also sampled the second transition – BR maroon to BR blue – during an exhibition with Grosvenor Square, but we've been hankering after more recent history too.

For this year's Yearbook project we decided to do something totally different again, but still with plenty of nostalgia. We've turned the clock forward to the ten-year period between 1995 and 2005 to create a West Coast Main Line themed layout fit for exhibition use. It was inspired initially by the impending arrival of Hornby's excellent Class 87 Bo-Bo overhead electric, which touched down in September, as well as the prospect of a brand-new Class 90 from Bachmann in 2019. However, once we got started we realised just how many memories both Mark Chivers and I had for the period and the route in the era we had chosen.

During that time I had many adventures to the northern section of the West Coast Main Line from my home in Yorkshire. That included day trips to Wigan and Crewe and longer trips which took in Oxenholme, Carlisle and Penrith. I also remember heading to Shap for a day trip after I'd moved south to see BR '8P' 4-6-2 71000 *Duke of Gloucester* tackle the ascent following restoration in the early 2000s. That was a great experience which also gave me the chance to see the last of the Class 87s on the West Coast

route as well as the newly introduced Class 390 Pendolinos, freight traffic in the hands of Class 60s and more.

As one of Britain's busiest railway lines (indeed, it is said to be amongst the busiest mixed-use railways in Europe) the West Coast Main Line is full of variety and in combination all this led us on a nostalgic voyage to try and create a fictional slice of the line. West Coast Cement is the result and we hope you enjoy discovering how we went about building it and seeing it on show in the coming months.

Of course there is much more to this Yearbook than just one layout build. We have our Top 20 products of 2018, a full review and listings for all the new locomotives and rolling stock released in 2017-2018 plus a detailed preview of more than 150 new products which are currently being developed for release in 2019 and beyond across three scales.

We also investigate the potential of narrow gauge modelling following the arrival of Bachmann's new Baldwin 4-6-0T for 'OO9', reflect on Grosvenor's first appearance in its new format, take you behind the scenes in the *Hornby Magazine* workshop with our 'O' gauge project layout, explore the world of hopper trains, show you how to weather Hornby Class 60s and upgrade a Heljan '47XX' 2-8-0 with sound. Plus you can read detailed historical features on the West Coast Main Line and development of the 'Atlantic' 4-4-2s while revelling in a selection of the very best layouts to be featured in the magazine over the past 12 months.

We hope you enjoy this feature packed eleventh edition of the *Hornby Magazine Yearbook*.

Happy modelling!

Mike Wild
Editor, *Hornby Magazine*

The late 1990s were a colourful period on Britain's railways with the sector liveried locomotives running alongside new schemes of privatisation. Class 87 87010 *King Arthur* hurries north with a rake of Virgin Trains liveried Mk 3s as Regional Railways liveried Class 37/4 37422 *Robert F Fairlie* heads south with EWS open wagons. Arriving at the cement works is 56003 in Loadhaul black and orange. Mike Wild.

HORNBY magazine TOP 20 OF 2018

Selecting a single stand out product from any year is a challenge, but in 2018 we've enlisted the assistance of *Hornby Magazine's* readers through the first annual *Hornby Magazine* Model Railway Awards to create our Top 20 of 2018.

Train-Tech automatic signals

- *www.train-tech.com*
- £40 each • 'OO' gauge

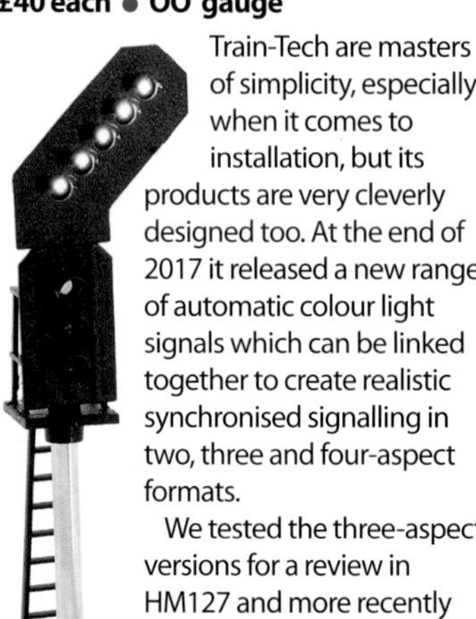

Train-Tech are masters of simplicity, especially when it comes to installation, but its products are very cleverly designed too. At the end of 2017 it released a new range of automatic colour light signals which can be linked together to create realistic synchronised signalling in two, three and four-aspect formats.

We tested the three-aspect versions for a review in HM127 and more recently

we have installed the four-aspect versions on our West Coast Main Line project layout to great effect. The range also includes mimic switches, which can be used to manually control the aspects, and more.

This clever range of signals also won the Innovation of the Year category in the *Hornby Magazine* Model Railway Awards.

- **Read the full review in HM127.**

Darstaed BR Mk 1 carriages

- *www.ellisclarktrains.co.uk* • £189 each • 'O' gauge

Coarse scale 'O' gauge manufacturer Darstaed made a move to finescale 7mm scale products in 2018 by introducing a new range of BR Mk 1 carriages through Ellis Clark Trains. The new range covers Brake Second Corridor, Second Corridor, Composite Corridor and several other vehicles in classic BR colour schemes from carmine and cream to maroon, green and blue and grey. More versions are coming too including the First Corridor, Restaurant Miniature Buffet, Gangway Brake and BR 57ft non-corridor carriages.

Their popularity saw these carriages take the Best 'O' gauge Carriage/Wagon award in the *Hornby Magazine* Model Railway Awards too.

- **Read the full review in HM130.**

Graham Farish Class 40 1-Co-Co-1

- *www.bachmann.co.uk* • £139.95 • 'N' gauge

The all-new Graham Farish Class 40 was selected as the Best 'N' gauge Locomotive in the *Hornby Magazine* Model Railway Awards. In fact, it only missed out on being part of the Top 20 of 2017 by a few weeks, as it came in just after Yearbook No. 10 had closed for press.

This standout new diesel model features a built-in cube speaker from the factory, a Next18 decoder socket, directional lighting and an impressive level of detail throughout. Our sample of D211 *Mauretania* was delivered in original BR green with disc headcodes while other versions were released with centre headcode boxes and split headcodes in BR blue.

With its powerful chassis, its performance on the track was just as good as its external appearance. Another worthy winner in the Model Railway Awards.

- **Read the full review in HM125.**

Locomotion Models' Stirling 'single' 4-2-2

● ***www.locomotionmodels.com*** ● **£239 (DCC ready), £339 (DCC sound fitted)** ● **'OO' gauge**

The Stirling 'single' is a beautiful locomotive. Built in 1870 at Doncaster Works for the Great Northern Railway, this elegant passenger locomotive was designed to haul the fastest trains on the southern section of the East Coast Main Line from London to York. In summer 2018 Locomotion Models delivered its eagerly anticipated ready-to-run model of No. 1.

The real locomotive forms part of the National Collection and Locomotion Models' new model is part of its National Collection in Miniature series – and what a model it is. Stunning attention to detail, wonderful decoration, a clever connection between the locomotive and tender, option for a DCC sound fitted version, two-axle drive through a complex gearbox and much more.

It is the model which captured the greatest number of votes in the Best 'OO' gauge Locomotive category in the *Hornby Magazine* 2018 Model Railway Awards, and rightly so.

● **Read the full review in HM133.**

Dapol four-compartment Maunsell Brake Third

● ***www.dapol.co.uk*** ● **£83.65 (three-car set)** ● **'N' gauge**

Dapol expanded its range of Maunsell carriages in 'N' gauge during 2018 with the addition of the four-compartment Brake Third. These were delivered in a collection of three-car sets modelling prototypical Southern Railway/Region carriage formations including the SR olive green set shown here. These finely appointed models gained the *Hornby Magazine* Model Railway Award for Best 'N' gauge Carriage/Wagon, as voted for by *Hornby Magazine* readers.

● **Read the full review in HM134.**

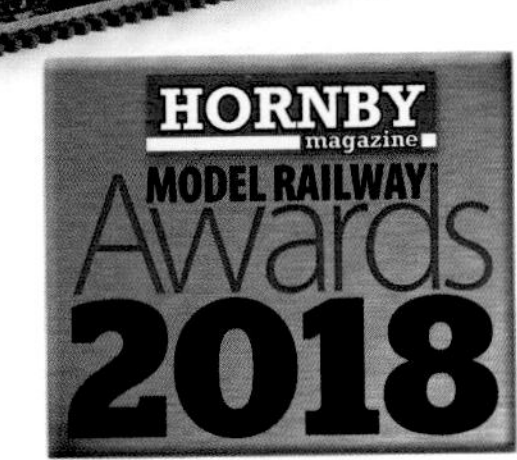

Bachmann FGA and FFA Freightliner flats

● ***www.bachmann.co.uk*** ● **£49.95 (FFA), £99.95 (FGA, pair)** ● **'OO' gauge**

Container traffic has always been a popular choice for modellers and manufacturers, but the longstanding five-vehicle Freightliner flats which were first introduced in 1966 have been missing from the 'OO' gauge ranges. Bachmann corrected that in autumn 2018 with the arrival of its FGA outer wagon pairs and FFA centre wagons for the scale.

We had the pleasure of inspecting a 1990s period set, which can be expanded with further FFAs to create an authentic five-wagon set. With their die-cast chassis, plastic details and superbly finished livery these new container wagons are sure to be very popular indeed. Bachmann has also produced a range of 40ft and 20ft containers to go with each wagon while an accessory pack includes clips to lock the containers in place, bufferbeam detail, wheel covers and more.

● **Read the full review in HM137.**

Dapol GWR '57XX' 0-6-0PT

● *www.dapol.co.uk* ● **£235 (DCC ready), £420 (DCC sound fitted)** ● **'O' gauge**

Winner of the Best 'O' gauge Locomotive category in the *Hornby Magazine* Model Railway Awards was Dapol's fine model of the GWR '57XX' 0-6-0PT. It debuted in May 2018 offering a brand new choice of ready-to-run motive power for 7mm scale, and one with some impressive features too.

Dapol's '57XX' comes with a flickering firebox effect, working inside motion, a removable cab roof for access to install a crew and is DCC sound ready with space for a 21-pin decoder and a 31mm round speaker underneath the chimney.

Moreover, this model runs and looks just as good as its specification suggested and it was a worthy winner of its title in the awards voting. Available in Great Western Railway, British Railways and London Transport colour schemes, if you are thinking of starting out in 'O' gauge or you already have a project on the go the '57XX' is a must have with great potential.

● **Read the full review in HM131.**

Hornby Wainwright 'H' 0-4-4T

● ***www.hornby.com***
● **£119.99**
● **'OO' gauge**

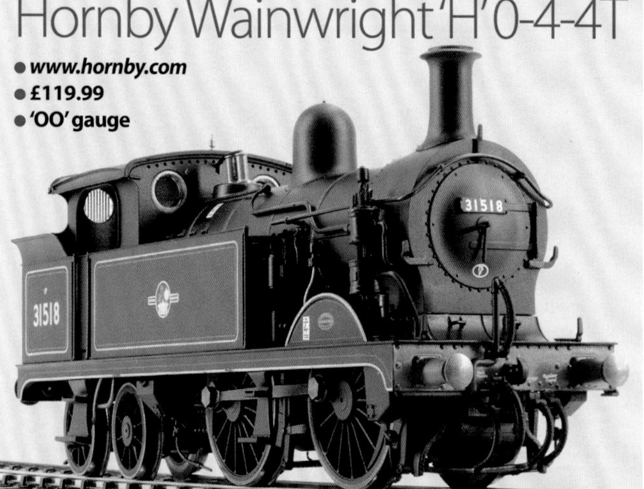

Hornby's delightful Wainwright 'H' 0-4-4T is another locomotive which just missed out on being part of the 2017 Top 20 listing as it arrived just a few weeks too late. Nevertheless, we had to include it this year as the manufacturer did a fantastic job in replicating the delicate lines of the South Eastern & Chatham Railway tank engine in 4mm scale. We even went as far as installing digital sound into one version for a feature in HM127 showing the full potential of the locomotive.

● **Read the full review in HM126.**

Heljan Class 07 diesel shunter

● ***www.heljan.dk*** ● **£139.00** ● **OO' gauge**

Southern Region subjects have been popular in 2018 and especially small 0-6-0 and 0-4-0s. Alongside the steam releases Heljan delivered its Ruston and Hornsby Class 07 0-6-0 diesel shunter. It was a quick seller in the shops, so fast in fact that within three months of its arrival Heljan announced another batch of nine new Class 07s for release in 2019.

The first batch covered both original condition and later air brake fitted locomotives in liveries ranging from BR green to BR blue and industrial schemes. Detail was excellent with a large number of separately fitted etched metal parts bringing the distinctive 0-6-0 shunter to life.

● **Read the full review in HM134.**

Hatton's SECR 'P' 0-6-0T

- ***www.hattons.co.uk***
- **£99.00**
- **'OO' gauge**
- **Read the full review in HM129.**

Hatton's Model Railways has been raising its game as a manufacturer of model railway products and, since 2017, it has been working directly with its factory to produce sought after models.

One of the highlights of the past 12 months was its delightful model of the South Eastern & Chatham Railway 'P' 0-6-0T. It was announced in summer 2017 and the first completed models were delivered to customers in March 2018. In total 12 versions were produced in the first batch covering SECR, SR, BR, industrial and preservation era colour schemes. More are on their way, offering modellers another chance to be a proud owner of a 'P' in 'OO'.

The level of detail on each was excellent throughout, including variances between locomotives, while the specification also included a five-pole motor, all-wheel pick-up, a 6-pin decoder socket and small tension lock couplings in NEM pockets.

Hornby Class 87 Bo-Bo

- **Read the full review in HM132.**

- ***www.hornby.com*** • **£170.99** • **'OO' gauge**

Overhead electrics have been in vogue of late with both Bachmann and Hornby developing new ready-to-run models to suit the West Coast Main Line. Bachmann's Class 90 is due in 2019, but Hornby's all-new Class 87 arrived in September in both original BR blue from the 1970s and 1990s period InterCity 'Swallow' colours.

The model carries off the boxy shape of the prototype superbly and Hornby has also gone to the lengths of modelling the detail differences between early and late period locomotives including different pantographs, central headlights and the addition of push-pull control jumpers on the later locomotives to suit their use with Mk 3 Driving Van Trailers.

The 87 comes with directional lighting (including a switch to change between day and night mode) an 8-pin decoder and a space for a 28mm round speaker below the PCB.

Bachmann LBSCR 'H2' 4-4-2

- **Read the full review in HM136.**

- ***www.bachmann.co.uk***
- **£189.95**
- **'OO' gauge**

The London, Brighton & South Coast Railway 'Atlantic' has been a long sought after model in 'OO' gauge and in October Bachmann delivered its highly anticipated release. Offering a finely detailed body, smooth running chassis, 21-pin decoder socket and space for a speaker, it ticked all the major boxes for a new product.

Originally set to model just the 'H2' 4-4-2s, in the end Bachmann decided to model the original 'H1' series locomotives too with three versions being released initially. These cover a LBSCR umber livered 'H1' together with 'H2s' in Southern Railway green and BR lined black.

Rails of Sheffield LNER Dynamometer Car

● *www.railsofsheffield.com* ● £125 ● 'OO' gauge

Rails of Sheffield delivered its 'OO' gauge model of the sought after London and North Eastern Railway Dynamometer Car in August and it has been extremely popular with the 1938 period model already sold out. It even went on to win the Best 'OO' gauge Carriage/Wagon category in *Hornby Magazine's* first annual Model Railway Awards in 2018 with a landslide 50% of the votes.

Produced by Rapido Trains for Rails, the Dynamometer Car features an exquisite exterior and interior, working lighting which can be controlled from a magnetic sensor and supplied 'wand' and a fully detailed underframe including the ninth wheel. It even went as far as modelling the different gangway connections at each end of the vehicle while including standard features such as turned metal wheels, sprung buffers and small tension lock couplings in NEM pockets.

Offered in both 1938 and post-1946 condition, the Dynamometer Car has far-reaching potential on 'OO' gauge layouts as it was used during the 1948 Locomotive Exchange Trials as well as for *Mallard's* record run in 1938 and many other occasions.

● **Read the full review in HM135.**

DCC Concepts Cobalt SS

● *www.dccconcepts.com* ● £49.95 ● All scales

DCC Concepts is no stranger to ingenious products and its new Cobalt SS point motors are another development in its line of high quality turnout power solutions. Cobalt SS is small, really small, measuring just 26mm x 20mm and features a stepper motor which connects to a highly capable circuit board to take care of all the point switching operations you could want. This includes frog switching, feedback and the option to add a manual switch to control the motors.

Meanwhile, control of the motor is sophisticated, allowing its throw length to be adjusted to suit any scale and design of point while a selection of hooks is included, again to suit different types and styles of point. Our first installation took about 20 minutes for a pair of motors including reading the instructions, but that will only improve now we know the processes involved. Highly useful for storage yards and, better still, no need to be underneath the baseboard during installation.

● **Read the full review in HM136.**

Dapol Class 68 for 'N' gauge

● *www.dapol.co.uk* ● £141.00 ● 'N' gauge

● **Read the full review in HM131.**

Dapol's 'OO' gauge model of the Vossloh Class 68 made it into our Top 20 of 2017 and its 'N' gauge model of the same diesel-electric is a very worthy addition to our listing for 2018. Delivered in April, the 'N' gauge Class 68 featured a stunning level of detail as well as directional lighting, a Next18 decoder socket and manual switches for lighting. Space for a speaker was designed into the chassis making this a fully prepared model whether you want to run it on analogue, digital or with digital sound.

Accurascale HUO 24.5ton hopper

● *www.accurascale.co.uk* ● £59.95 ● 'OO' gauge

A new name in ready-to-run rolling stock – Accurascale – launched its first British outline wagon in the summer: the BR HUO 24.5ton hopper. This finely detailed hopper wagon was designed to suit drop-in wheelsets to 'EM' and 'P4' gauges while each was factory fitted with 16.5mm gauge 'OO' wheelsets.

With its excellent detail, both inside and outside the hopper, and variety of livery finishes it ticked a lot of boxes. In addition, Accurascale delivered enough wagons with different running numbers to allow a 15 wagon train to be produced without repetition. TOPS versions have now been released while the manufacturer is working on a HUO for 'O' gauge together with a Cemflo and PCA cement wagon for 'OO' gauge with more to come.

● **Read the full review in HM134.**

Bachmann Baldwin 4-6-0T

● *www.bachmann.co.uk*
● £149.95 ● 'OO9' gauge

Bachmann made British outline narrow gauge mainstream in 2018 with the arrival of its Baldwin 4-6-0T to suit 'OO9' gauge railways. The locomotive followed the same manufacturer's new 'OO9' bogie wagons, which arrived in late 2017, providing a catalyst for a new breed of narrow gauge modellers.

In the past 'OO9' has required the use of overseas prototypes or kit building, but the launch and expansion of Bachmann's ready-to-run product range for the scale (along with a growing range of rolling stock by Peco) is opening up narrow gauge modelling to a wider audience. Excellent news.

● **Read the full review in HM131.**

Absolute Aspects banner repeater

● *www.absoluteaspects.com* ● £60.00 ● 'OO' gauge

Specialist Absolute Aspects produces an outstanding range of signals for model railways in 'OO' and 'O' scales with one of its recent innovations being production of a fully working banner repeater signal for 4mm scale. Better still, it has been designed to be paired with the manufacturer's range of signals so that it mimics the aspect shown by the main signal, just as on the real railway.

Available post mounted and as a head only suitable for mounting on bridges or buildings, this impressively detailed signal offers something totally different for signalling schemes which will introduce more realism too.

● **Read the full review in HM128.**

Hatton's 'Warwell'

● *www.hattons.co.uk* ● £85.00 ● 'O' gauge

The past 18 months have been a busy period for ready-to-run 'O' gauge wagons. In 2017 Dapol launched its BR 12ton vent vans and 10ton open wagons while in early 2018 it brought the Lionheart Trains BR 16ton mineral wagons back to the market. Minerva was active too with its models of the GWR 'Iron Mink'.

Hatton's joined the 'O' gauge rolling stock club too with its attractive model of the LMS 50ton bogie 'Warwell' wagon which offered something rather more distinctive. As with their 'OO' gauge model of the same wagon the 7mm scale version was produced in both early condition wagons with diamond frame bogies and post 1970s vehicles with Gloucester GPS bogies while the plastic deck was supported by a die-cast frame. A superb model which deserves strong sales.

● **Read the full review in HM129.**

Heljan GWR '61XX' 2-6-2T

● *www.heljan.dk* ● £699 ● 'O' gauge

Heljan is well known for its 'O' gauge diesels and it has now broken into the steam market for 7mm scale with the arrival of its GWR '61XX' 2-6-2T. This impressive model captures the bulky design of the GWR 'Large Prairie' with fine detailing, purposeful motion and a superbly detailed cab interior.

The model has also been designed to be more DCC friendly than the twin motor diesel locomotives by the inclusion of a LokSound L4 decoder interface to suit the manufacturer's sound decoders. Speaker provision is in the chassis, but there are other options within the body to enhance any potential sound output.

With its top-notch performance – aided by a powerful flywheel driven five-pole motor – the '61XX' is an attractive mid-sized locomotive for 'O' gauge which will sit neatly alongside Dapol's new '57XX' 0-6-0PT.

● **Read the full review in HM137.**

West Coast CEMENT

UNDER CONSTRUCTION

This year the *Hornby Magazine* team selected the West Coast Main Line in the late 1990s as the subject for the Yearbook project layout. **MIKE WILD** introduces this new 20ft x 10ft exhibition layout and explains how it has been developed.

Hornby Class 60 60033 *Tees Steel Express* rumbles along the main line with a rake of empty PCA cement wagons destined for the exchange sidings. In the background the dual carriageway is busy with passing traffic.

THE WEST COAST Main Line (WCML) is one of Britain's busiest main lines and a major freight artery from London to Birmingham, the North West and Scotland. Stretching north from Euston station in London it takes in fast four-track main line sections in the south leading to a winding and challenging double-track route after Crewe through the northern fells to reach Carlisle. It is this latter section that we chose to base our new project layout on, set somewhere between Lancaster and Carlisle in a fictitious location.

In the past the majority of *Hornby Magazine's* layout projects have been set in the 1950s and 1960s with the exception of West Riding Power (HM Yearbook No. 8), which modelled the early 1980s. For this project we wanted to model a different period selecting the colourful time between 1995 and 2005. This 10-year period covers the final years of British Rail and the transition into privatisation. It offers a wide variety of colour schemes with the arrival of the shadow privatisation freight companies – Loadhaul, Transrail and Mainline – alongside the outgoing InterCity, Railfreight triple grey and a number of special one-off liveries. Plus it saw the introduction of EWS maroon and gold, Virgin Trains and many more as privatisation took hold.

Another inspiration for the project was the impending arrival of the Hornby Class 87 which made its debut in September. This is to be followed by the Class 90 from Bachmann in March 2019 providing two brand new overhead electrics fit to lead a West Coast Main Line fleet. Of course, Class 87s and 90s means installing overhead catenary – a challenging prospect – so right from the start we aimed to keep the track plan for the main line section simple.

Recycled cement

The starting point for this layout was a plan to rebuild Felton Cement Works to give it a new lease of life. The project started in May for a feature in HM132 which saw the original cement works board stripped of its single track main line but retain its original yard plan and buildings. The original station board for Shortley Bridge (HM Yearbook No. 7) was then stripped back to bare board to complete the straight scenic section providing a 12ft running line. The overhead masts were assembled on the cement works board first over a new double-track main line laid with Peco code 75 concrete sleeper track.

After a break to complete other layout projects, the part-completed 12ft section was brought back into the workshed and the original corner storage yard boards were stripped of their »

track and added to each end to extend the full scenic frontage to 20ft x 2ft. The trackplan was then developed to feature a double-track main line with a goods loop on the inner circuit at the front with a long thin cement works site behind. The exchange sidings in the cement works were laid to accommodate a 20-wagon cement train and locomotive allowing long trains to be brought into the yard for shunting through the loading point.

From the start the layout was to be operated by Digital Command Control (DCC) and its simple track layout for the main line means that all the points on the scenic section will be switched using accessory addresses on the DCC handsets. Gaugemaster's Prodigy Advance system is being used to power the layout with separate power buses for the main lines and points. Point motors on the scenic section are Peco solenoid motors powered by a DCC Concepts AD8-Sfx eight-output accessory decoder.

As a main line scene, we also wanted fully working four-aspect colour light signals too – and a type which could operate without manual intervention except when needed. For this we turned to the Train-Tech automatic signalling range and four four-aspect colour lights have been installed on the layout. These have sensors to trigger the signals to change to red when a train passes and they then work through the sequence of yellow, double yellow and back to green. Better still the signals can be linked together so that they work as they would on the railway. For example, as a train passes over a sensor the previous signal is linked so that it will show a yellow aspect while the next is at red. When the red changes to yellow the previous signal changes to double yellow and when the yellow aspect signal changes to double yellow the previous signal changes to green, just as on the real railway.

Another useful feature is that each can be controlled with a DCC address as well which is particularly useful at the junction as the joining line can be held at red while the main line operates automatically. Similarly the main line signal in this instance can be set to red to allow the junction

Capturing a busy West Coast Main Line scene Hornby Class 87 87010 *King Arthur* races south with a rake of Hornby Virgin Trains liveried Mk 3 stock while a Cross Country HST set speeds north. In the cement sidings a Loadhaul Class 56 has just arrived with a fresh set of wagons for loading.

signal to be cleared using the DCC address to allow a train to join the main line from the goods loop. Completing the signalling setup is a Train-Tech DCC fitted ground signal which will give trains a clear route out of the cement works when appropriate.

All of these signals are powered by the DCC track supply and we have altered each of the four-aspect signals to take away the legs which are designed for fitment under the rails to take power and to allow the sensor connections to be taken below the baseboard. Train-Tech has designed them to be as simple as possible to install and the only reason we chose to complicate things is to take the wiring for them below the baseboard (see guide below).

Modelling the modern railway also meant we needed concrete cable runs alongside the main lines which we added using the Wills kits' parts together with relay boxes from the same source at each signal and, where possible, orange cable passing underneath the track to link signals back to the concrete cable trunking.

Underneath the baseboard, the wiring is relatively simple for West Coast Cement. Two power buses run the length of the layout – one for track power, the other for point power – installed using 28/0.2 (28 strands of 0.2mm wire) figure of eight cable for a quick installation. Track feeds were made with red and black 7/0.2 equipment wire and joined to plug-in terminal blocks at each baseboard join as well as the power bus. A third wire also runs the length of the layout to connect the sensors on the two outer circuit colour light signals.

Overhead electrics

The Peco code 75 concrete sleeper track was laid in our usual way. Gaugemaster 1/16in cork was laid across the boards first followed by the track which was pinned in place with Peco ST-280 track pins. The cork was then cut back to the edges of the sleepers to allow a ballast shoulder to be formed at the next stage. Wire droppers were soldered to track sections as required next to allow the full trackplan to be weathered and ballasted.

As we were using concrete sleeper track, our weathering method involved painting the rail sides with Lifecolor Track Grime by brush before ballasting with a combination of Woodland Scenics fine and medium grade blended grey ballast. This was applied with a Proses ballast spreader before being brushed into place and then glued down with diluted PVA wood glue in a 50:50 ratio with water and a drop of detergent added to take away the surface tension from the water. Before glue application, the ballast was wetted with a water mister to stop it moving during the process.

With ballasting complete we could move on to installation of the overhead masts for the catenary. This had already been completed in front of the cement works, but it left another 14ft of overhead to install. All of the masts and wire spans are from Peco's range of overhead equipment produced by Somerfeldt.

The masts required 3mm holes to be drilled through the baseboard using the supplied jigs in the starter pack made by Somerfeldt for Peco. These jigs are invaluable for quick and accurate installation of the masts and by using suitable wire spans the position of each mast can be located correctly.

Having installed the masts, the brackets and registration arms which support the wire spans were soldered on to the masts. Soldering to the Peco catenary masts requires a soldering flux to ensure a strong joint. We used DCC Concepts flux throughout soldering of the overhead catenary including joining the wires spans to the masts. Once you have understood and practiced the process, installing the overhead spans is straightforward, if time consuming.

Buildings

Fortunately the majority of the buildings for the cement works were already complete. Felton Cement Works used the Walthers Valley Cement kit as its basis with buildings modified to fill the full length of the backscene as low relief structures. Included in the scene are a set of storage silos, a loading point, manufacturing buildings and a conveyor. »

MODIFYING TRAIN-TECH SENSOR SIGNALS

As delivered the Train-Tech sensor signals are designed to be plug and play. The two prongs slide under the rails between the sleepers to take power and position the sensor correctly alongside the track.

To allow the sensor wiring on our signals to pass underneath the baseboard we unsoldered the three-pin plug from each signal's circuit board. This needs to be done carefully to avoid any damage to surrounding tracks on the board.

We then connected a yellow wire to the central pin (which can be used to connect to a mimic switch in the future if required) and a blue wire to the rear pin to link through to the next signal to control sequencing of the signal aspects.

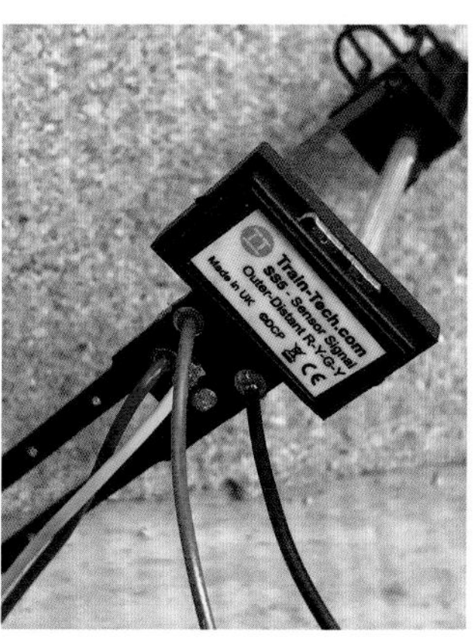

Rather than use the prongs to collect power we soldered red and black wires to the optional DCC power connections on the circuit board.

The prongs were then cut back to the markers on the legs completing modification of the wiring of the signal prior to installation.

Two 2mm holes were drilled for the red and black wires and a pair of 2.5mm holes were joined together for the blue and yellow wires to pass through the baseboard. The orange wire here is cosmetic.

The signal was then glued in place on top of a small square of cork to make it level with the trackbed. The black and red wires were then connected back to the DCC power bus and the blue wire linked through to the next signal as per Train-Tech's instructions.

To bed each signal in, ballast was added around its base and over the circuit board ensuring that the sensor was kept clear of obstructions. This completed the installation of each signal.

UNDER CONSTRUCTION

West Coast Cement recycles the majority of the baseboards from Shortley Bridge and Felton Cement Works. The original cement works board was retained with modifications to the track while the original station board was cleared back to bare wood for the new layout.

The original corner boards from the storage yard were used to make the new corners for West Coast Cement. This meant lifting and recovering the track and point work from the boards, much of which will be used in the new storage yard for the West Coast layout.

Mark Chivers applies diluted PVA glue to the freshly laid ballast after spraying it with water to assist the flow of glue.

The main line plain track on West Coast Cement is Peco concrete sleeper track with code 75 rail.

Ballast spreading was carried out with a Proses ballast spreader. This speeds up the process of laying ballast, but it still needs brushing into place before gluing.

Train-Tech four-aspect colour light signals have been used for all the main line signals. Here we are testing the signals before modifying the wiring as described in the separate panel on page 15.

The cement yard tracks were weathered with Humbrol No. 29 from an aerosol can while the concrete sleeper track had the rail sides brush painted with Lifecolor Frame Dirt.

A combination of Wills modern industrial units and a scratchbuilt loading dock and low relief building make up the extension to the cement works.

Ballast was added around the loading dock to bed it into its surroundings. The roller doors in the scratchbuilt building are from the Wills range.

Static grasses start to bring depth and texture to the ground cover around the railway.

The cement works buildings were weathered with DCC Concepts limestone weathering powder with highlights of white and rust. This is the early stage of the weathering process – the colours being further blended together after this image.

Approaching completion – more ground cover is required, one more building left to weather and bedding in of the road bridge to be completed with Woodland Scenics fine leaf foliage.

Extension of the cement works area from its original 6ft x 2ft footprint meant we needed more buildings, but we had already exhausted the components of the kit in the original build. Instead we used a combination of scratchbuilding using Wills corrugated iron sheets and roller doors from the same manufacturer's modern range. We also used Wills modern warehouse and extension kits to create a series of low relief buildings along the rear of the layout.

To expand traffic potential further in the cement works, we also added a loading dock in front of the long scratchbuilt bagging building using 2mm thick plasticard to allow bagged cement to be loaded into VGA four-wheel and Cargowaggon bogie wagons.

All of the new buildings were painted with Halfords grey primer before weathering with DCC Concepts Limestone weathering powders to give them a lived in look. This was applied with a large flat brush and worked across all surfaces.

The other major civil engineering project on the layout was the creation of a dual carriageway crossing the railway as a scenic break at the left-hand end of the layout. Originally we had thought of a motorway bridge, but the space required for six lanes of traffic plus hard shoulder and central reservation would have taken up too much space. Instead we decided to downgrade the road to a dual carriage way – still a large structure at 235mm wide – which contains two lanes of traffic in each direction and a central reservation.

The structure for the bridge was built from 6mm MDF and raised 100mm above the baseboard to clear the railway and overhead masts. The structure was then clad in Evergreen Plastics 1mm thick plasticard which was scored to represent concrete panels. Evergreen 'I' section plastic strip was added underneath the roadbed to represent the supporting structure for the bridge while a series of 12mm round columns were added between the main line and cement works headshunt in similar fashion to modern road bridges that we have seen.

All of this was then sprayed with Halfords grey primer before the concrete sections were finished off with a top coat of Woodland Scenics concrete paint and weathering with Geoscenics Black Concentrate applied with an airbrush and then brushed into streaks with a large flat brush. The »

DUAL CARRIAGEWAY ROAD BRIDGE

The dual carriageway road bridge hides the curves as trains enter the scenic section at the left-hand side of the layout. The base is built from 6mm MDF with the same material used for the deck. It is set 100mm above the baseboard to suit our layout design and to clear the overhead masts. The width of the deck is 235mm. It has been joined together with panel pins and PVA wood glue.

A set of five 12mm diameter round supports have been added using dowelling rod. These were fitted in place using screws and PVA wood glue.

To add extra detail under the road deck we added a series of Evergreen 8mm 'I' beam sections (Cat No. 278) to represent the support structure for the road above. These were glued in place with multi-purpose contact adhesive.

The outside of the bridge structure and the inner walls were clad with Evergreen 1mm thick plasticard sheet (Cat No. 9040). This was scored to represent concrete panels modelled using photographs of a real motorway bridge.

road surface was painted with Woodland Scenics ashphalt paint colour while road markings will be added from the Busch range.

Ground cover

With its industrial backdrop and main line railway scene the space left for ground cover, apart from ballast, is quite limited on West Coast Cement. The base colour for the grassed areas is Woodland Scenics fine blended green turf which has then been overlaid with static grasses from MiniNatur and Green Scene before finishing with more blended green turf and coarse turf in light green and burnt grass colours. Static grasses were also used around the cement works to bed in the railway to its surroundings.

Completing the ground cover is Woodland Scenics fine leaf foliage which was used to bed the motorway bridge into the raised ground as well as adding the finishing touches around the loading dock and other scenic structures.

Future development

What you see here is the first phase of development for West Coast Cement as there is a fourth baseboard to complete scenically ahead of its debut at the Warley National Model Railway Exhibition on November 24/25 2018 when it will be shown on the *Hornby Magazine* stand.

This board will include a level crossing across the main lines and cement works branch together with a cutting leading to the scenic break. The level crossing will use Wills' new modern level crossing kit with twin barriers which we are modifying to include Train-Tech working level crossing lights at the viewing side. These will be controlled by an accessory

Class 37/4 37422 *Robert F Fairlie* leads a short four-coach Regional Railways working past the cement works while Class 56 56095 *Harworth Colliery* ticks over in the yard.

The finishing touches were 7mm deep strips of 1mm thick plasticard for the sides, 12mm wide strips along the edges and a 25mm strip along the centre to represent the central reservation.

The whole bridge structure was then removed for painting. It was sprayed with Halfords grey primer first to seal the wood before being finished with Woodland Scenics Concrete Paving colour (Cat No. ST1454).

To keep road traffic on the bridge, Scale Model Scenery safety fencing was added along the outer edges. Gaugemaster roadside crash barriers (Cat No. GM381) will be added along the central reservation.

address so that the lights go through the correct sequence before a train passes through.

There is also further detailing to complete around the cement works, detailing of the ground cover and construction of a new modular storage yard which can be used with future scenic frontages to expand the *Hornby Magazine* layout portfolio.

We are already looking forward to taking West Coast Cement out to exhibitions and after the Warley show at the NEC in Birmingham its next planned outing is the 2019 Great Electric Train Show on October 12/13 at the Marshall Arena in Milton Keynes. Keep watching in *Hornby Magazine* for the latest information on the layout and more news on its next adventures. ■

USEFUL LINKS	
Evergreen	*www.hattons.co.uk*
Gaugemaster	*www.gaugemaster.com*
Green Scene	*www.green-scenes.co.uk*
Peco/Wills	*www.peco-uk.com*
Woodland Scenics	*www.bachmann.co.uk*
Train-Tech	*www.train-tech.com*

● Turn to pages 76-83 to learn about the stock roster for West Coast Cement.

Ground cover around the bridge was built up using cardboard formers covered with a web of masking tape. This was later covered with squares of newspaper coated in PVA glue on both sides to make a lightweight and strong land form.

The bridge sides were then weathered with Geoscenics Black Concentrate – let down with water and sprayed through an airbrush. This was then streaked down the concrete panels. The last painting step was to paint the road surface with Woodland Scenics Asphalt Paving colour (Cat No. ST1453).

WHAT WE USED

Product	Manufacturer	Cat No.
1mm thick plasticard sheet	Evergreen	9040
2mm thick plasticard sheet	Evergreen	9080
8mm 'I' beams	Evergreen	278
3ft x 2ft 1/16in cork sheet	Gaugemaster	GM130
Spring and summer medium static grasses	Green Scene	Various
Catenary starter pack	Peco	LC-100
Single catenary mast	Peco	LC-110
260mm catenary wire spans	Peco	LC-151
340mm catenary wire spans	Peco	LC-152
380mm catenary wire spans	Peco	LC-153
500mm catenary wire spans	Peco	LC-154
Track pins	Peco	ST-280
Code 75 track with concrete sleepers	Peco	SL-102F
Code 75 large radius right-hand point	Peco	SL-E188
Code 75 large radius curved left-hand point	Peco	SL-E187
Code 75 medium radius right-hand point	Peco	SL-E195
Code 75 medium radius left-hand point	Peco	SL-E196
Code 75 track with wooden sleepers	Peco	SL-100F
Code 75 metal rail joiners	Peco	SL-110
Code 75 insulated rail joiners	Peco	SL-111
Corrugated iron plastic sheets	Wills	SSMP216
Industrial retail unit extension	Wills	SSM315
Industrial unit	Wills	SSM300
Roller shutter doors	Wills	SSM313
Concrete cable trunking	Wills	SS87
Relay boxes	Wills	SS85
Relay boxes	Wills	SS88
Concrete Paving paint	Woodland Scenics	ST1454
Asphalt Paving paint	Woodland Scenics	ST1453
Medium grade blended grey ballast	Woodland Scenics	WB1394
Fine grade blended grey ballast	Woodland Scenics	WB1393
Blended green fine turf	Woodland Scenics	WT1349
Light green coarse turf	Woodland Scenics	WT1363
Burnt grass coarse turf	Woodland Scenics	WT1362
Medium green fine leaf foliage	Woodland Scenics	WF1131
Olive green fine leaf foliage	Woodland Scenics	WF1133
Lightweight Hydrocal casting plaster	Woodland Scenics	C1201
Four-aspect sensor signal starter kit	Train-Tech	SSP1

A 'TUG' TRANS

With little more than waterslide transfers, a bottle of meths, a set of etched nameplates and a lick or two of paint, **TIM SHACKLETON** reworks three EWS Class 60s into a condition suited to their final days in traffic.

EVERYONE LOVES the 'Tugs', as the Brush Class 60s are often known – well, perhaps not accountants or maintenance engineers or signallers who've had one 'sit down' on them with rush hour fast approaching. But to enthusiasts (for their scarcity value and photogenic good looks) and drivers (for their raw power and unrivalled adhesion) the Class 60s are very special indeed.

I first caught a glimpse of one at Eastleigh in Trainload Construction livery when brand new, quickly followed by a much clearer sighting of 60054 *Charles Babbage* at Cricklewood. I was captivated, an impression reinforced by every one I've seen since. The spectacle of so many of them in the charnel house of Toton's Old Bank sidings was pretty grim but at the opposite extreme was my first glimpse of a DBS red 'Super 60' barrelling along with an oil train, seen through pouring rain from the A1 north of Newark. This was the first I knew of the reincarnation of one of my favourite classes, and the equally vibrant new livery in which the '60s' had been turned out. To say it was an agreeable surprise was understatement on an epic scale.

This piece is about the class in its final days of ordinary service, before the lucky ones went red while others from the Toton mausoleum were sold off to Colas and subsequently passed to GBRf. Inevitably, Hornby's 'OO' gauge model is the basis of the project – this, in my view, is unquestionably the best ready-to-run diesel ever released, and only Dapol's Class 68 comes even remotely close to this standard. Because of the all-round excellence of detail, finish and especially performance I found little to do to my as-bought, out-of-the-box models – instead, their transformation is achieved through sympathetic weathering (copied as always from prototype photographs) and the use of aftermarket products such as transfers, almost all of which were supplied by Railtec Models of Belper, Derbyshire. Upgrades on this scale don't need to cost much and, even if they did, it would still be worth it just to have three locomotives that, in their own unique ways, stand out from the common herd. I hope this piece inspires you to attempt similar customisations among your own fleet. ■

FER-MATION

Gone but very far from forgotten – 60020 and 60044 went on to form part of the 'Super 60' project, while 60021 was eventually acquired by Colas. Traditional depot scenes such as this have almost vanished from the prototype, which is why modelling has such an important role to play in recreating the past.

STEP BY STEP WEATHERING AND DETAILING HORNBY CLASS 60S IN 'OO'

1 A pair of Hornby Class 60s, one with the original EW&S lettering and the other in the later, subtly different style. Otherwise the two models are identical. They convey brilliantly the feeling of power and purposefulness evoked by these 70ft long, 129ton, 3,100hp machines.

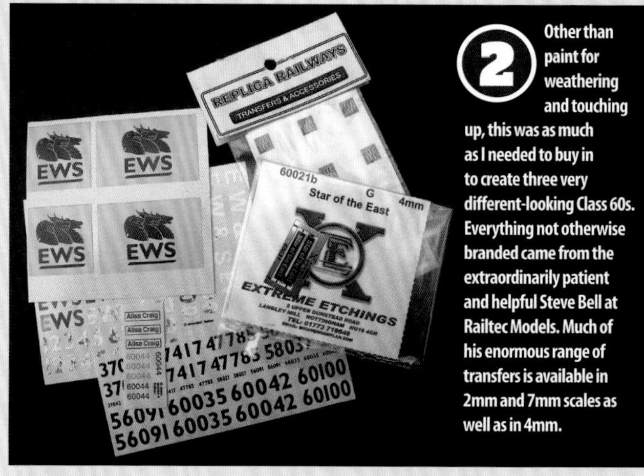

2 Other than paint for weathering and touching up, this was as much as I needed to buy in to create three very different-looking Class 60s. Everything not otherwise branded came from the extraordinarily patient and helpful Steve Bell at Railtec Models. Much of his enormous range of transfers is available in 2mm and 7mm scales as well as in 4mm.

3 I wanted to renumber my three '60s' in any case – wherever possible I like to model locomotives I've photographed and represent them in the condition seen in my pictures. There's nothing wrong with the solid EW&S logo and number, but I wanted the scruffy, faded lettering that many of these locomotives bore in the 'noughties.

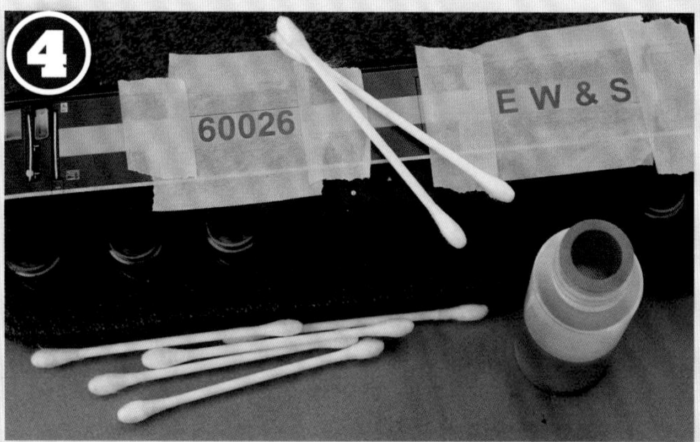

4 The first step was to use masking tape to protect areas of the bodyside that I didn't want to be affected by the methylated spirits I was using to remove Hornby's tampo-printed lettering.

5 Gentle rubbing with a cotton bud soon gives this result. Keep the bud moist but don't overdo it, or you might stain the paintwork. An initial application of meths gets things moving, then charge another cotton bud and take off the majority of the unwanted colour. A third application with a fresh bud should shift any remaining residues.

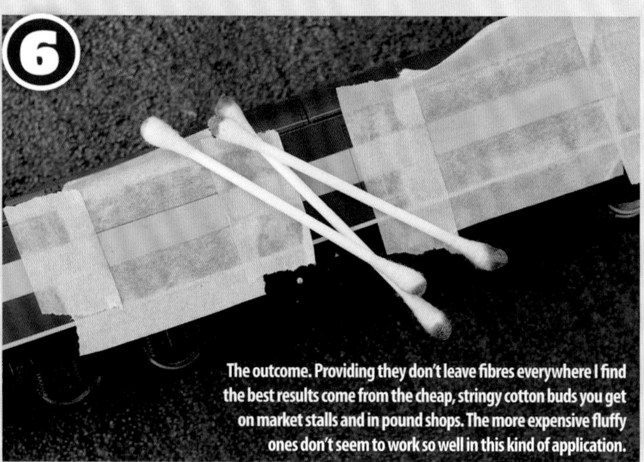

6 The outcome. Providing they don't leave fibres everywhere I find the best results come from the cheap, stringy cotton buds you get on market stalls and in pound shops. The more expensive fluffy ones don't seem to work so well in this kind of application.

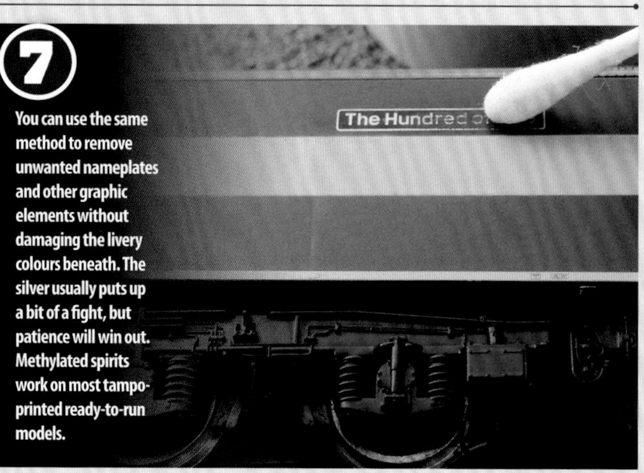

7 You can use the same method to remove unwanted nameplates and other graphic elements without damaging the livery colours beneath. The silver usually puts up a bit of a fight, but patience will win out. Methylated spirits work on most tampo-printed ready-to-run models.

Another shot that helped kick-start this project – on January 16 2008, early EWS-liveried 60020 brings an infrastructure train through Hatfield & Stainforth, bound for Doncaster. I'm a great fan of the grubby workaday railway and go out in all weathers to photograph it. Nice clean locomotives on perfect summer days aren't really my scene.

It didn't take long – half an hour at the most – to end up with a blank canvas on which to create the future *Star of the East*. If you've been heavy on the meths you may end up with a white deposit that can either be washed off with tap water or, depending on the form it takes, carefully incorporated into the weathering effects.

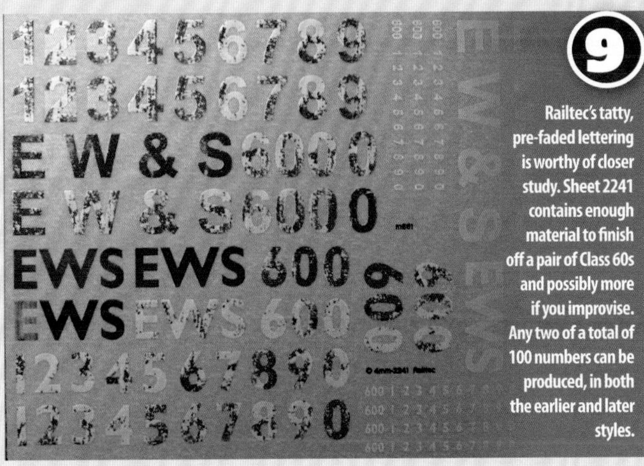

Railtec's tatty, pre-faded lettering is worthy of closer study. Sheet 2241 contains enough material to finish off a pair of Class 60s and possibly more if you improvise. Any two of a total of 100 numbers can be produced, in both the earlier and later styles.

Although I've barely started on the weathering, you can see how effective the faded, ghostly graphics are. On some EWS-liveried '60s' in their final years they were completely white, adding to the aura of neglect and official indifference long associated with the 'Tugs'.

STEP BY STEP WEATHERING AND DETAILING HORNBY CLASS 60S IN 'OO'

11

At Barnetby one dull March morning back in 2007, my eye was drawn to someone's finger having traced the name of 'A3' 4-6-2 60066 *Merry Hampton* on the grubby bodyside of this similarly-numbered 'Tug'. A decade later I copied the effect by scraping the name of 'A4' 60020 *Guillemot* on my equally shabby-looking model of 60020. The torn EWS 'big beastie' sticker was also useful future reference.

12

Now to apply the heavy-weathering treatment to a Mainline-branded Class 60. Just three of them – 60011, 60044 and 60078 – carried the so-called 'Aircraft Blue'. The silver lining was already starting to look more than a touch cloudy when, some time after acquisition by EWS, the logos vanished behind large yellow stickers. I distressed the striping using methylated spirits as before and at the same time removed the Mainline logotype, in case it showed through.

13

I pre-weathered the bodyside by fading the blue livery using a pale, warm-coloured wash – in this case a Light Grey panel line wash from Mig Ammo (A-MIG 1600) applied with a broad flat brush in vertical streaks.

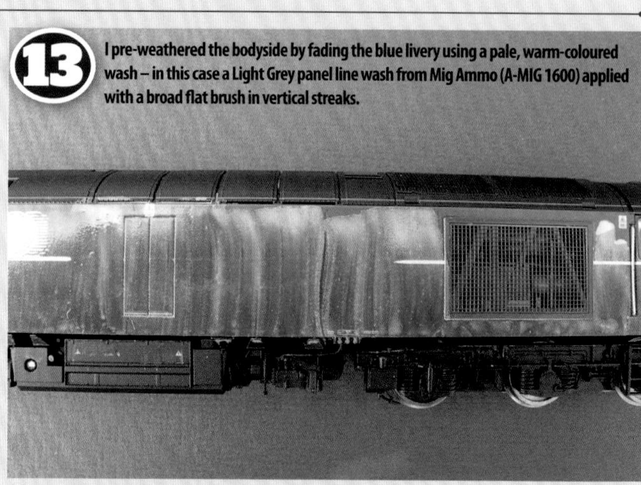

14

Using minimal quantities of white spirit, I took most of the wash off, again using vertical brushstrokes. This simple treatment has the effect of gently toning down the base colour and can be used with any livery (yellow, for instance, or bright red) that fades and softens with exposure to sunlight. Darker reds and greens, on the other hand, tend to blacken with age.

15

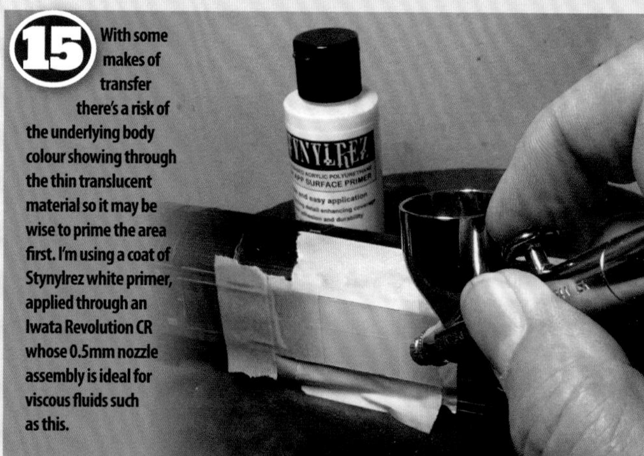

With some makes of transfer there's a risk of the underlying body colour showing through the thin translucent material so it may be wise to prime the area first. I'm using a coat of Stynylrez white primer, applied through an Iwata Revolution CR whose 0.5mm nozzle assembly is ideal for viscous fluids such as this.

16

While I had the roll of masking tape out – I use Tamiya because it doesn't tear the surface beneath – I got ready to paint the silencer assemblies. Whatever the class of locomotive, these are always rusty and soot-blackened. I used Tamiya Flat Black (XF-1) let down with Red Brown (XF-64), a combination that took me back to the days when I used Humbrol Metalcote Gunmetal and Matt Leather as the basis of almost all my weathering.

17

I used combinations of the same two colours to weather down the underframes and lower bodysides of all three 'Tugs'. Apart from Tamiya's own thinners, the only generic brand I can find that works with their paint is Ultimate. The roofs of Class 60s seem to be washed down quite frequently so you need to be sure plenty of the original colour shows through, however heavy the exhaust staining may be around the silencer.

Beginner SKILL LEVEL Intermediate Advanced

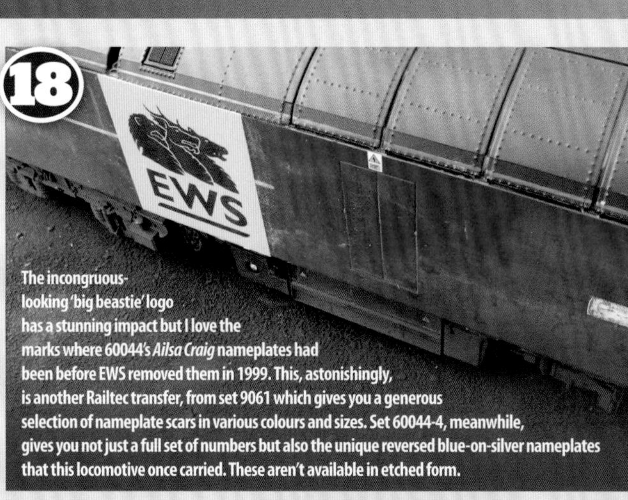

The incongruous-looking 'big beastie' logo has a stunning impact but I love the marks where 60044's *Ailsa Craig* nameplates had been before EWS removed them in 1999. This, astonishingly, is another Railtec transfer, from set 9061 which gives you a generous selection of nameplate scars in various colours and sizes. Set 60044-4, meanwhile, gives you not just a full set of numbers but also the unique reversed blue-on-silver nameplates that this locomotive once carried. These aren't available in etched form.

In later days the paint on the aluminium window frames wore away, exposing the metal beneath. This is an effect well worth replicating but in my view nothing looks less like metal than metallic paint. Instead, I touched them in with a very pale grey, Lifecolor Hellgrau (UA603). Being an acrylic paint, the inevitable blobs and blemishes can be rubbed away with a wooden cocktail stick.

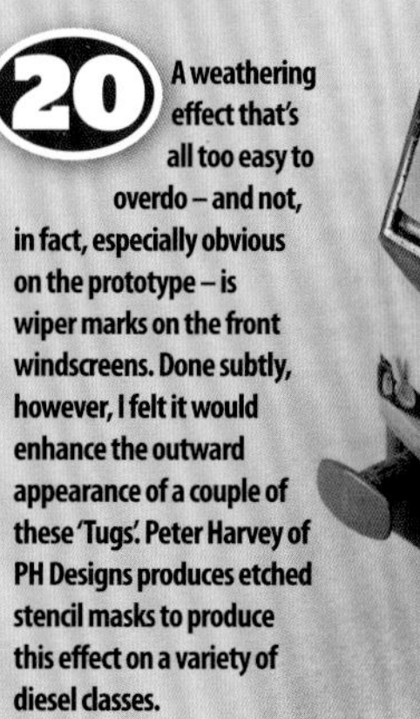

A weathering effect that's all too easy to overdo – and not, in fact, especially obvious on the prototype – is wiper marks on the front windscreens. Done subtly, however, I felt it would enhance the outward appearance of a couple of these 'Tugs'. Peter Harvey of PH Designs produces etched stencil masks to produce this effect on a variety of diesel classes.

The wiper marks need to be as understated as you can possibly make them. To avoid overcooking it I suggest using a quality matting agent such as Testor's Dullcote rather than paint. The effect isn't caused by dirt so much as the central portion of the windscreen being polished by the wipers so it's much shinier than other areas. You see this on car windscreens too, even though the vehicle is otherwise clean and tidy.

I've been photographing trains for close to 60 years and it never ceases to amaze me how a shot taken many years ago can one day instigate a modelling project. Here on a bitterly cold and misty December 22 2006, EWS/Mainline-liveried 60044 – the former *Ailsa Craig* – brings Teesside steel through Milford Junction. This was one of the pictures that inspired this article.

WHAT WE USED

PRODUCT	MANUFACTURER	CAT NO.
Class 60 windscreen wiper masks	PH Designs	PH4W1L
Light Grey panel line wash	Mig Ammo	A-MIG 1600
Stynylrez white primer	Scale Model Shop	SNR-401
10mm masking tape	Tamiya	87031
Flat Black acrylic	Tamiya	XF-1
Red Brown acrylic	Tamiya	XF-64
Hell Grau acrylic	Lifecolor	UA603
BR Maroon acrylic	Lifecolor	UA615
Dullcote	Testors	Testors Dullcote

STEP BY STEP WEATHERING AND DETAILING HORNBY CLASS 60S IN 'OO'

22 Progress with 60021 *Star of the East* – many (but certainly not all) EWS repaints had maroon-coloured cabside window frames rather than the black usually carried. I'm not sure about other ready-to-run manufacturers but the closest match I've found to Hornby's factory-applied shade is LifeColor BR Maroon (UA 615), applied with a long-bristled No 1 brush. The unique Railfreight Petroleum vinyls carried by this locomotive are from Replica Railways.

23 Some Class 60s stayed presentable to the end – with their slab sides they would have been easy to clean in mechanical washing plants. While avoiding an unlikely box-fresh finish, this is the condition in which I wanted to portray *Star of the East*. Hornby's factory paintwork is excellent. I spruced things up with a brush-painted application of Winsor & Newton 'Galeria' satin varnish, which scales nicely whereas the gloss version is a little too shiny for my taste. Nameplates are by Shawplan, secured with a few spots of body-coloured paint.

24 60020 meanwhile shows the typical fading of locomotive numbers and logos which was common on the Class 60s. These have been recreated with Railtec Transfers while the weathering has been produced using Tamiya Flat Black (XF-1) and Red Brown (XF-64).

25 60044 has been given a heavier weathering to match its condition in my photograph from December 2006. The EWS 'big beastie' logo stands out on the Mainline blue paint scheme, but makes this model unique amongst the crowd.

26 The three 'Tugs' lined up on shed – I can almost smell the exhaust fumes and hear the big Mirrlees engines on tickover. This is another variation on the theme of depot dioramas that we explored more fully in the HM121 issue of *Hornby Magazine*.

More bad weather – I didn't have a decent picture of *Star of the East* (the name coined by the Great Central Railway's publicity department for its newly-opened deep-water port at Immingham) so the next best thing I could find was 60071 *Ribblehead Viaduct* not too far away at Barnetby on May 4 2012, with empties returning from Jarrow. Other than the ones destined to become 'Super 60s', operational members of the class were thin on the ground by this date.

USEFUL LINKS	
Railtec Transfers	*www.railtec-transfers.com*
Hornby	*www.hornby.com*
Replica Railways	*www.replicarailways.co.uk*
Tamiya	*www.tamiya.com*
Lifecolor	*www.airbrushes.com*
Extreme Etchings	*www.shawplan.com*
Stynylrez (UK supplier)	*www.scalemodelshop.co.uk*
PH Designs	*www.phd-design-etchings.co.uk*

Left: **Close-up of the effects of time and the weather on a Class 60 – it's not just a brown wash along the lower bodysides! This is very much the kind of picture that, rather than deleting, I file under the 'might come in useful one day' category. It certainly did.**

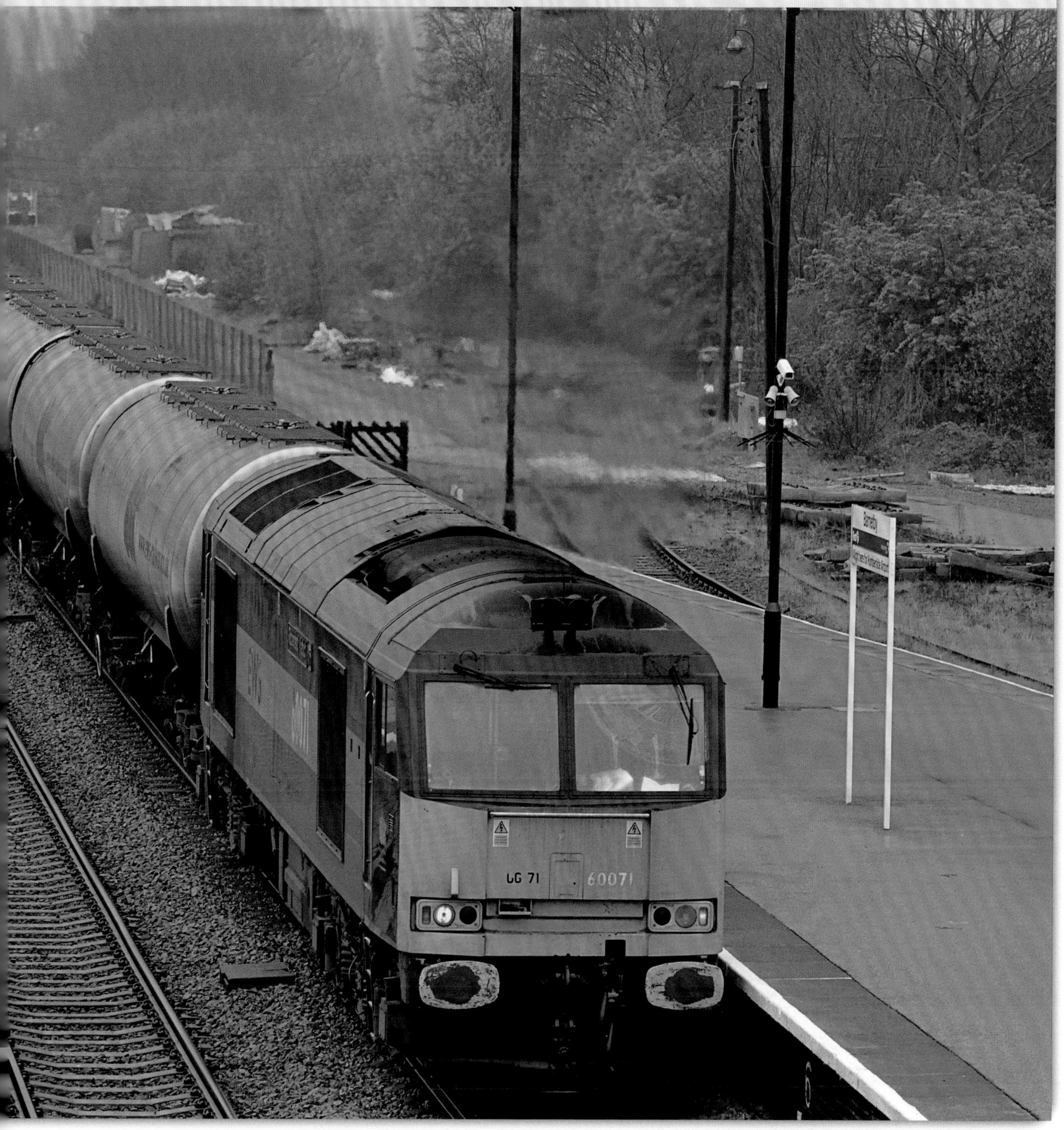

Buckingham GREAT CENTRAL ...a working railway

Before DCC, flexible track and today's vast range of models there was Buckingham. Far from being a museum piece, the trains still run regularly on this 'EM' gauge layout that has been a massive influence on modellers for 70 years. **TONY GEE** explains what makes operating Buckingham so magical.

Rush hour at Buckingham. These four trains all leave between 4.27pm and 4.57pm. Nearest the camera is a 'special'. In Edwardian times, the gentry could hire a train for their own personal use and this one is moving horses, carriages and people (in a luxury saloon carriage) from the family's country house to their London home. The other trains terminate at Grandborough - two loaded with horse boxes - work through to Leighton Buzzard and form a semi-fast service for Marylebone.

TO ANY MODELLER OVER THE age of 40, amongst the most inspirational model railways ever built is the Reverend Peter Denny's Buckingham branch. It was started in the late 1940s and Peter was still developing it when he died in 2009. Comparatively few people saw the layout in the flesh because, after some early appearances at the Model Railway Club's Easter show, it had found a permanent home at Peter's vicarage in Cornwall and was never again exhibited to the public. Its reputation was mostly founded on a steady stream of articles and, in particular, on photographs of the layout published in the modelling press.

What these could never convey, however, was the experience of operating Buckingham. It may have been good to look at, it may have been a platform for revolutionary ideas on all manner of topics – from locomotive building and rotary storage yards to hand-scribing brickwork and modelling trees – but make no mistake, Buckingham was a model railway designed to run, and to be run in as prototypical a manner as possible. It even boasted a homemade electro-mechanical computer at a time when only the largest commercial organisations were exploring the possibilities of computerisation.

Over the years I've been very active in building and exhibiting layouts and I've also had the opportunity to operate some of the best-known train sets in the country. None, however, has given as much pleasure as Buckingham. I'd got to know the workings of the layout quite well following numerous visits while Peter was still alive and in 2011, thanks to the kindness of Peter's family, the layout was moved to a purpose-built shed in my garden. With much help from friends, it's gradually been brought back to working order.

It won't be many years before youngsters will be asking "What is coal?" but in 1907 it provided most of our industrial and domestic energy. Buckingham alone has a delivery of six loaded coal wagons every day. Three are for the coal yard pictured here, two for the gasworks and one for the locomotive shed, carrying special high quality steam coal.

Far from being a museum piece preserved behind glass, it's now 90% functional. Other than some essential rewiring, pretty well everything is exactly as it was when Peter had the layout, with the same stock, the same track plan, the same timetable – and the same imaginative and highly personal solutions to perennial modelling problems.

Control system

In the normal course of events we operate Buckingham twice a week. We start at whatever point we left the timetable last time and run the layout for two or three hours. As Peter always maintained, regular operation is good for the layout. It keeps electrical contacts polished and the more we use it, the better it performs. Large or small, if you want your railway to run well, then run it!

A major factor is the reliability of the electrical »

This lovely locomotive – GCR '11A' 4-4-0 269 (LNER 'D6') – is now 70 years old and still runs week in week out, usually taking turns on the slip coach workings. It is approaching Grandborough Junction on its way to Buckingham. The carriages seen here were converted many years ago from Tri-ang GWR Clerestories and are the only ready-to-run stock on the layout. Peter Denny was one of the first finescale modellers to appreciate the possibilities that proprietary models could offer.

switching system which, quite simply, is the best I've ever seen. Although Buckingham is a comprehensive terminus, with a 69-lever frame, there are virtually no section switches. As one operator succinctly put it: "Who needs DCC?" On Buckingham, the track supply is arranged through switches on the signal levers. Pull the right signal and power goes to the track from the correct controller. For example, if you are marshalling stock within the station, shunting signals apply power from the Buckingham controller to the track. If a train is departing, you offer it to Grandborough Junction using your block instruments. If the operator can accept it – but not before – you set the points and clear the signals. Power on the relevant tracks is transferred to the Grandborough controller and the operator there drives it away from Buckingham.

Once the locomotive of a departing train has cleared the end of the platform, the starting signal can be returned to danger and the locomotive trapped at the buffer stops can follow the departing train up the platform using the Buckingham controller. Trains coming into Buckingham are worked in a similar way, with the signal at Grandborough Junction transferring the down line to the Buckingham controller. This is accomplished not by DCC but by homemade switches made from brass or phosphor bronze wipers nailed to the wooden sliding lever frame. I've learned a great deal about how to wire a layout from Buckingham and my next layout – while fully embracing more recent technologies – will incorporate quite a number of these lessons.

There are a few switches, especially at Grandborough Junction where locomotives may need to be isolated to allow the pilot to add or remove vehicles from a train. In addition, both Buckingham and Grandborough have a second controller that allows you to switch over various groups of sidings so shunting can be performed while trains are running under separate control on the main line. These days you can do all this with DCC but Peter still managed to achieve a great deal of sophistication using conventional analogue control, due in no small part to his extraordinary imagination and willingness to experiment. And there are fewer buttons to push, doing it his way.

Similar switching arrangements exist between Leighton Buzzard and Grandborough Junction. Of late Leighton Buzzard, which we've occasionally been able to take to shows in recent years, has been away for overhaul and branch trains from Buckingham, instead of running through, temporarily terminate at Grandborough. No doubt some dreadful horse-drawn bus substitute then bumps its way along dodgy roads to Leighton Buzzard – after all, it is 1907. The amazing thing is, operation has hardly suffered as a consequence.

A railway system

The entire Buckingham system is contained within an area just 17ft x 14ft, but the pleasure of operating is greatly enhanced by having no fewer than four stations on the layout, all of them entirely imaginary (the Great Central never reached any of these places). The main terminus and locomotive facilities are at Buckingham. The operational hub, with two junctions and a small marshalling yard, is Grandborough Junction. There's a smaller terminus at Leighton Buzzard plus the tiny Bourton Halt between Grandborough and Buckingham. In addition, there's a vestigial branch from Grandborough to Verney Junction, which ends in a short tunnel and is served by a push-pull train. The storage yard, meanwhile, is a six-track turntable and every so often the timetable has an instruction to turn it round. Otherwise, very little interaction goes on there and none of the locomotives are handled at any stage.

Such a system gives us the opportunity to run

properly timetabled train services, with regular connections between trains. At intermediate points, anything from coal to livestock is dropped off and added before making its way to a variety of destinations. Some passenger trains only go as far as Grandborough – how many layouts do you see where trains terminate and are reversed at through stations? It happens all the time on the prototype, but almost never on model railways.

All the locomotives and stock work for a living, and operations are highly railway-like in a way that's seldom seen on exhibition layouts where simply keeping something running is often enough. To keep the paying public happy, trains emerge at frequent intervals from the storage yard, do a circuit of the track and then go back to their place in the storage sidings. If it's a terminus layout, the train arrives, the locomotive runs round and promptly goes back whence it came. There may be a sequence, but it's rarely a timetable.

Terminus-to-storage-yard layouts with simple in-and-out operation have always been popular. This is part of the pattern at Buckingham too but there is so much more. In my view, the thing that really sets the railway apart is the intricacy and intensity of the operation. Even workings that could be simple and straightforward are turned into fascinatingly complex patterns purely through the thought that Peter Denny put into creating the timetable. At any given moment the majority of the stock on the layout will be on the move, being marshalled or reformed, standing at a station platform or in a goods yard awaiting loading and unloading. The locomotives, and there are far fewer of them than you might imagine, don't stand around doing nothing for long and no train spends more than an hour or so, if that, parked in the storage yard. There are some trains that never visit the off scene yard at all!

The layout was designed for three operators, Peter and two of his sons, Stephen and Crispin. One operated Buckingham, one Grandborough and the third, usually Crispin, ran Leighton Buzzard and the storage yard. When the layout is working to its full capacity, it has a couple of operational modes. Control of the storage yard is by a wonderful electro-mechanical device called the 'Automatic Crispin' (or AC for short). In the normal course of events it communicates directly with the operator at Grandborough Junction. Fully renovating this extraordinary robot-like contraption is still on the 'to do' list, but the automation has the timetable on an acetate roll and will offer and accept trains just like a real operator would. For one-man operations, the 'Automatic Crispin' – so called because it replaced the real Crispin when he wasn't available for running sessions – can be made to work directly with Buckingham, giving a basic storage-yard-to-terminus operation. The other stations are, in effect, switched out.

One or two people, familiar with the layout only from photographs or track plans, have commented on how close the stations are to each other. But when you sit at the Buckingham control panel, Grandborough is behind you out of sight (and vice versa) so the fact that it is only a scale quarter-mile away becomes irrelevant (the real places are seven miles apart). You exchange bell codes, you see a train depart off scene and that's it. What's happening six feet away is of no concern to you – you have more than enough to keep you occupied as it is. No operator can see the whole of the layout at once and with experienced hands at the controls, communication between sections is entirely through block instruments.

Running to time

From the very early days of Buckingham through to today, the layout has been operated to a strict timetable. Reflecting the railway practice of the period, it uses the 12-hour convention. Initially the layout was worked as a sequence of moves and later, a speeded-up clock was introduced whereby an actual minute is condensed into about 40 seconds of 'Buckingham time'.

Like most things on Buckingham, the clock (which is still regularly used) was a wonderful creation put together from odd bits of wood and Meccano gears – nowadays, digital clocks with variable speed would avoid the need for such a »

What Buckingham, and our great hobby generally, is all about – operators immersed in the running of the layout and transported back to 1907. All we are thinking about is collecting a horse box from the siding and all the troubles of the modern world are forgotten.

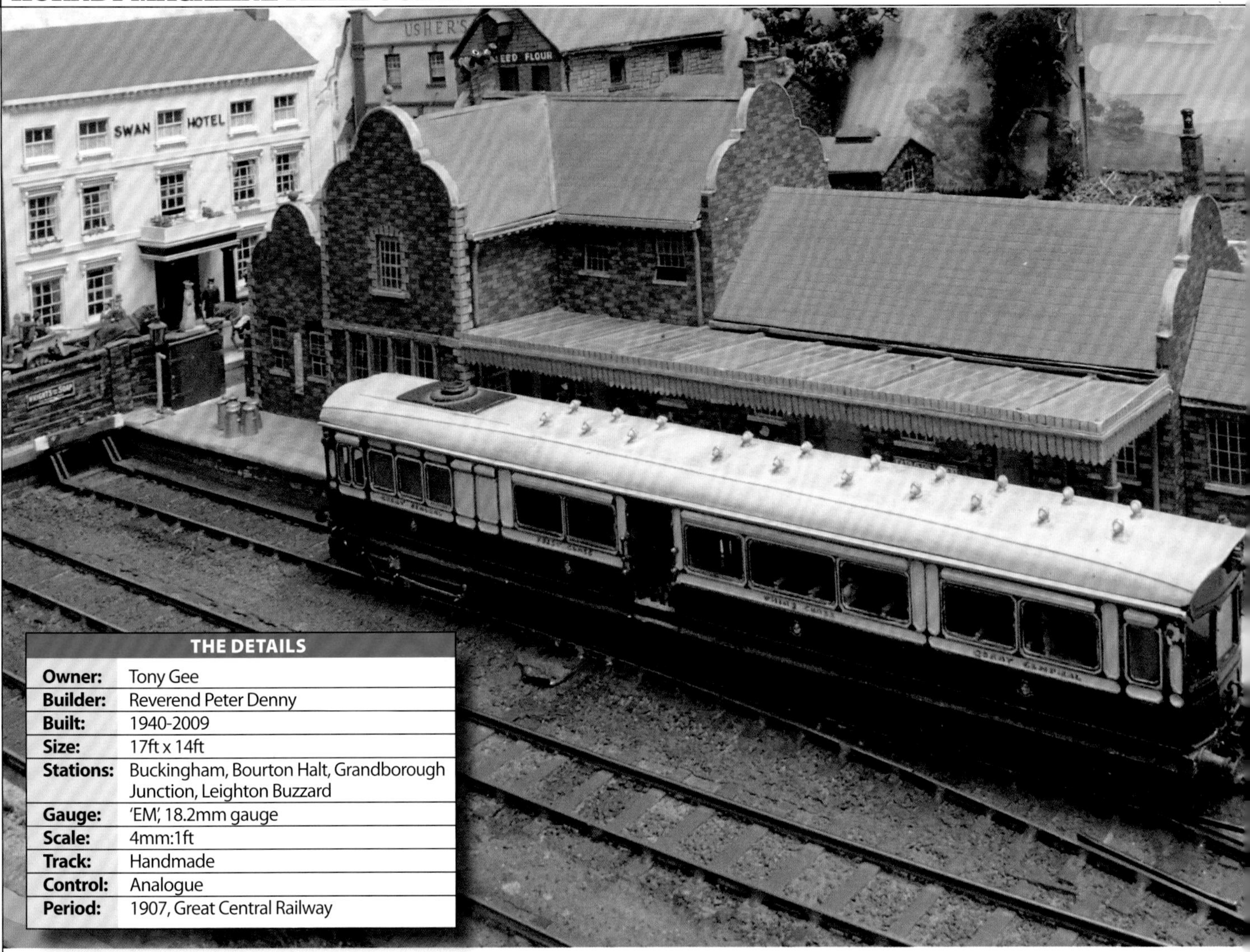

THE DETAILS	
Owner:	Tony Gee
Builder:	Reverend Peter Denny
Built:	1940-2009
Size:	17ft x 14ft
Stations:	Buckingham, Bourton Halt, Grandborough Junction, Leighton Buzzard
Gauge:	'EM', 18.2mm gauge
Scale:	4mm:1ft
Track:	Handmade
Control:	Analogue
Period:	1907, Great Central Railway

device. Later still, the clock became part of the Automatic Crispin, so that the whole operation of the railway becomes a challenge of keeping up with the clock. If the operators fall behind, the 'AC' will stop the clock – this was to be avoided if at all possible as it was seen as a black mark against the operators.

Conversely, there is a great deal of satisfaction in running the layout with the clock and keeping up with it. As we said, the timetable has around 100 moves that take about eight hours to work through. Early in the morning and late in the evening, there are large gaps between trains but at other times (we have genuine rush hours!) even the slickest of operators is under real pressure to get trains turned around and out of the platforms. The sense of achievement when it all goes well is very pleasing but at times it can all get a bit intense.

Running to the clock not only adds greatly to the realism but also gives you a certain amount of planned shunting time. If you know the next train isn't due for 20 minutes, there's scope to organise the goods yard, turn and prepare locomotives on shed for their next duties, add vehicles to or remove them from trains standing in the platforms and all the other little duties that happen on Buckingham but not, I suspect, on many other layouts.

So sometimes we run to the clock and sometimes we don't, but one thing we rarely do is turn around and ask the other operators: "Are you ready for me to send the cattle train?" They don't work like that on 12in:1ft railways and we don't on Buckingham. Real railways used various methods, including the bell and block instruments built by Peter Denny to offer and accept trains. Some people find this sort of thing a bit over the top, but it adds another slice of authentic working practice to the operation of the layout. As a case in point, Peter preferred not to refer to the storage yard as a storage yard – in the timetable, the correct destination is always quoted, and trains terminate at or originate from Marylebone, Aylesbury or Quainton Road rather than the storage yard.

Passenger trains

So, we have a well-designed layout with several stations. We have the highly effective design of the electrical systems. We have a timetable and we know which trains we should be running, which locomotives should be on them and where they should go. We have a railway-like way of sending trains from one place to another. But all this would be pretty much redundant if all we did was despatch trains from one end of the layout to the other and back again.

For our 100-move timetable, we have a grand total of three main line bogie carriage sets, two rakes of six-wheeled carriages, a branch set (for Leighton Buzzard), a steam railmotor and the push-pull set. We do sometimes get an extra passenger train as one of the bogie sets has the facility to slip a carriage at Grandborough Junction (yes, Buckingham has a working slip coach). The beauty of the operation is that trains do different things each time they run and it simply doesn't register that you're seeing the same set of vehicles in a subtly different guise – passenger trains with or without horseboxes and parcels vans, for instance, or goods trains that

Buckingham gas works. Peter did a lot of research to allow him to build a believable model of a gas works and he enjoyed it so much he built two more. Each station now has one and apart from being attractive and unusual scenic features, they create traffic for the railway – coal inwards and outward traffic in the form of empties, coke, tar and other by-products.

When Peter rebuilt Leighton Buzzard in the late 1960s, he based it on an early version of Buckingham station. He never threw anything away and a number of buildings made redundant by previous modifications found a new lease of life. These include the lovely station building seen here, with the railmotor about to depart for Buckingham, calling at Grandborough and Bourton Halt.

An overall view of Grandborough Junction. This section of the railway is the only one that has remained substantially unaltered throughout the layout's existence – largely, I suspect, because from an operational point of view as well as an aesthetic one it couldn't be bettered. The shunters are busy sorting out the cattle train and a local passenger service is just pulling in to Platform 3. The locomotive, unusually, is one that Peter Denny didn't build. He needed a locomotive to haul the Director's saloon (it hauls passenger trains between such duties) and I was delighted to be asked to build it for him.

Grandborough Junction shed, with the station pilot resting between duties. Freight locomotives stable here but it's never an especially busy place, unlike the main depot at Buckingham. The depot looks like it's been extended at some time – a nice touch, as so many of these places often were. In fact Peter built it this way because he liked the look of the saw-toothed roof. A single pitched roof, he felt, would have been out of touch with the simple character that always prevailed at Buckingham.

are remarshalled en route and split into portions for different destinations. This is why the yard at Grandborough Junction is so fascinating to work, while the Buckingham pilot is also kept busy round the clock.

I will use the slip coach as an example. It works from the fiddle yard (Marylebone or Oxford) through to Buckingham several times during the day. Initially, it runs as a stopping passenger, pausing to pick up and set down at Grandborough. Some while later it forms part of a non-stop express that sometimes passes straight through Grandborough Junction and at other times drops off the slip carriage, using a home-made coupling worked by a ramp. The slip coach then becomes a single-coach train that has a varied set of duties. Once a day it works up to Leighton Buzzard. On another run, it is purely for the convenience of passengers wishing to alight at Grandborough and it waits there until it is re-attached to a train later in the sequence, having been shunted to a siding in the yard for a while. When it works to Buckingham, it creates a nice little task for the station pilot, which has to reassemble the train with the slip coach at the rear before it can set off again.

Another example is the Verney Junction push-pull train. It could spend its time running from Grandborough into the little dead-end tunnel and back again. But no, it uses different platforms to make connections with other trains and sometimes goes on to the storage yard and at others doesn't, taking it on to a fresh section of track through open countryside beyond the junction. The timetable is all recorded in handwritten charts, with individually printed 'turnover' cards at each station. It is lovely to see all the alterations made over the years, with bits of tape, Tippex and different inks, all in Peter's own hand.

There are two trains, meanwhile, that never leave the scenic section – the steam railmotor and the Leighton Buzzard branch train. I think they were among Peter's favourite models and hiding them away off scene would have kept them out of view. Instead they spend all day shuttling between Leighton Buzzard, Grandborough and Buckingham and also serve Bourton Halt. Again, sometimes they work through, sometimes they terminate at Grandborough and the branch set hauls a variety of tail loads to keep the shunters busy and vary the appearance of the train.

Freight workings

The goods trains are equally diverse and interesting to run – a fitted non-stop goods with fish and perishables, an early morning milk and newspaper working, an engineers train, a horse box special, a pick-up goods that spends the day shuffling from Leighton Buzzard to Buckingham, shunting at Grandborough on the way. A cattle train sets off each day from Buckingham, it's always market day in the county town, with livestock. A number of cattle vans are dropped off at Grandborough Junction, some of which will make their way to Leighton Buzzard while the rest of the train travels further afield.

There is a daily freight to and from London, which conveys wagons that form the backbone of local goods services. All the wagons have a »

A portrait of a fine model of a fine locomotive. Sacre 4-4-0 430B was built in the 1870s and the last were not withdrawn until the early days of the LNER. Peter Denny was born when they were still running and that gives me a feeling of direct connection to the railways of that time.

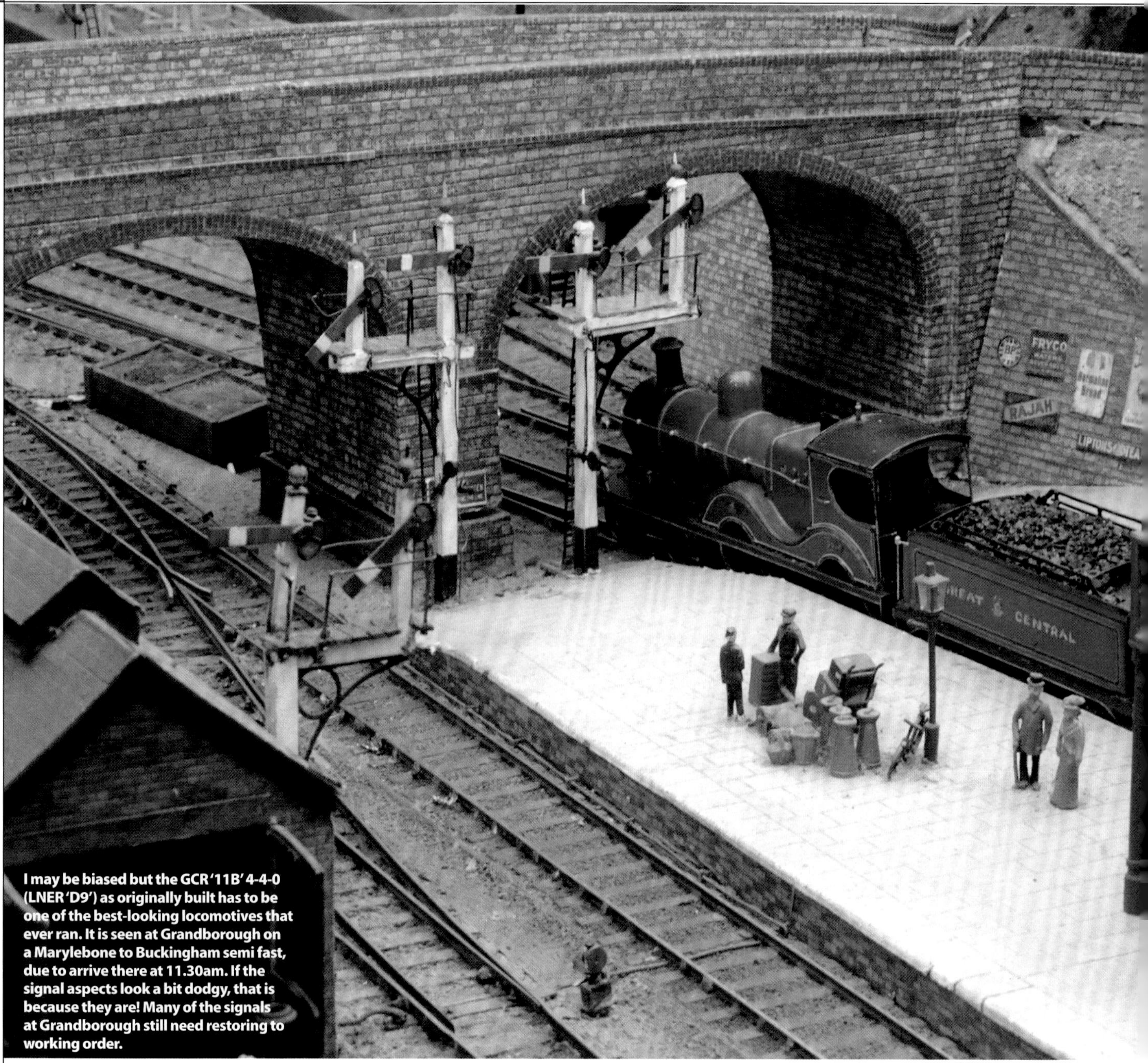

I may be biased but the GCR '11B' 4-4-0 (LNER 'D9') as originally built has to be one of the best-looking locomotives that ever ran. It is seen at Grandborough on a Marylebone to Buckingham semi fast, due to arrive there at 11.30am. If the signal aspects look a bit dodgy, that is because they are! Many of the signals at Grandborough still need restoring to working order.

coloured dot on the solebar at the right-hand end, there being eight colours in all. Charts at Grandborough and Buckingham show what happens to the wagons with particular dots on each day. In the marshalling yard at Grandborough, there are specific sidings for wagons destined for different parts of the layout. A peg in the charts tells you if you are on day 1, 2 or 3 as on each run through the timetable, the colours change. It is simple to set up, simple to work and, if you're so minded, turns shunting from merely pushing a few wagons about into a real brain-teasing challenge. Experienced shunters follow the example of their real-life counterparts by sizing up the best way of sorting a given group of wagons with the fewest number of moves in the fastest possible time. As well as greater operational efficiency this means less legwork and more time to get the kettle on.

At the start of the day, meanwhile, there are empty coal wagons dotted all over the layout that are gradually assembled into a long rake of empties, which head off 'up north' to collieries served by the Great Central Railway. When they reach the storage yard, the empty wagon bodies are swapped for fulls and in due course a loaded train arrives at Grandborough yard and the wagons are systematically dispersed to various destinations, including locomotive coal to the sheds as well as the gasworks and the coal drops at Buckingham. This body swap is the only time we need do anything in the storage yard other than turn it round.

We're still finding new ways to shunt the trains but operators still get caught out when, not thinking ahead, they turn the page and suddenly see the notice "with horse box". At this point the yard foreman has to swing into action to find an empty one in a siding, get it shunted over to the loading bank and ensure it's attached to the front of the train, where all loaded horse boxes should be marshalled.

Enjoyment

Having worked with the timetable for around six years, I still haven't memorised it and there's no sign of us growing bored with working the same sequence of trains over and over again. Although we've come close, once, we've never yet worked through the full eight-hour, 100-train sequence in one hit. Generally speaking we're happy to do

A quiet moment at Grandborough, with shunting completed and the pilot taking a breather. How many have sidings purely for sorting trains for different destinations? Not many, I would suggest – the yard may be compact but its size is out of all proportion to its usefulness. The signalbox is one of my favourite buildings on the layout. It is full of character and charm and just looks so right in its location.

a couple of hours or so and then leave the WTT open at the page ready for another group of operators to take the layout through the next set of moves.

I know that this way of running a model railway isn't for everybody. I understand there are people who're happy just watching a succession of trains pass by but I wonder if they're missing out on a big part of the hobby, the joy of operating a layout rather than simply running trains. This was what model railways were all about in Peter Denny's day but in recent years the 'parade of trains' layout seems to have taken over.

So I hope this account has shown how applying a bit of imagination to the operation of a layout can add a whole new dimension to 'playing trains', as well as significantly increasing the enjoyment and satisfaction that ensues. Even if Buckingham had been built entirely from off-the-shelf models with ready to lay track, it would still be a superb layout to operate. The fact that it was all built from scratch, by one remarkable man, just makes it all the more special.

It only remains for me to thank my regular operators – Alan Rollins, Chris Wright and Laurie Adams – for making our twice-weekly sessions so fulfilling and such good fun. ■

The cattle train has been made up in the yard at Buckingham and a locomotive brought from the shed to take it to Grandborough and then Aylesbury. Today it is in the capable hands of one of a pair of Robinson 'J11' 0-6-0 goods engines on the layout. It leaves here full, delivers cattle to various destinations on and off the layout and then the empty wagons are stabled overnight in the yard at Grandborough.

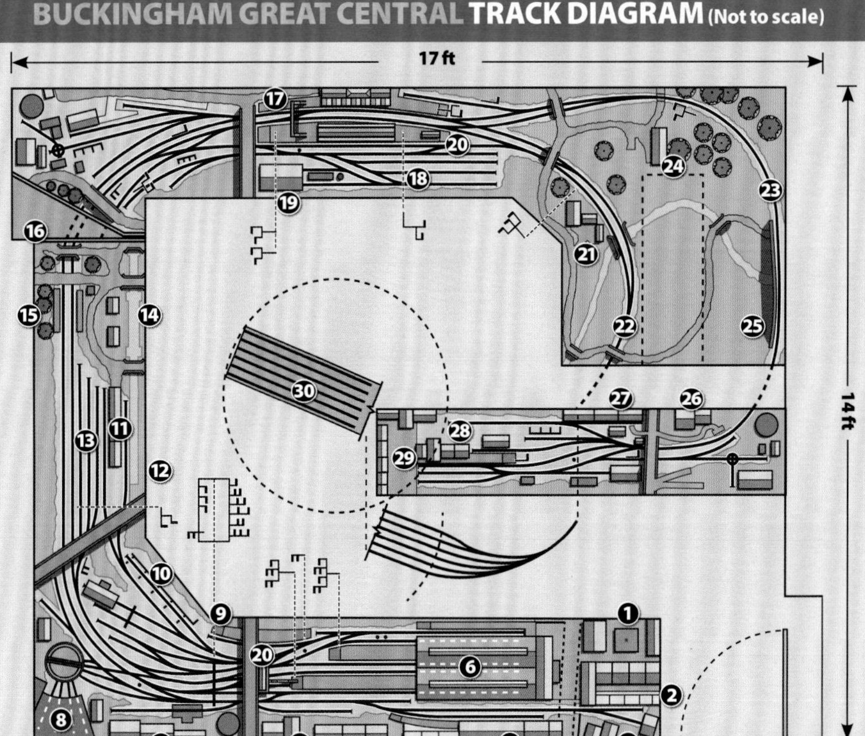

KEY

1. Market Square
2. Cattle pens
3. Maltings
4. Goods warehouse
5. Shops and houses
6. Buckingham Central station
7. Gas works
8. Engine shed
9. Perishable goods depot
10. Coal drops
11. Wharf
12. Builders yard
13. Carriage sidings
14. Canal lock
15. Bourton Halt
16. Scenic break
17. Grandborough Junction station
18. Goods yard
19. Engine shed
20. Signalbox
21. Farm
22. Main line to Marylebone
23. Branch to Leighton Buzzard
24. Manor House
25. Viaduct
26. Flour mill
27. Paper mill
28. Leighton Buzzard Linslade
29. Station buildings
30. Storage yard

Two years ago we started a new project to build an 'O' gauge test track which has the dual purpose of providing a location for testing new models as well as being home to **MIKE WILD's** collection of locomotives and rolling stock. Here he explains how it has been developed and the plans for its future.

1 'Warship' D869 *Zest* draws out of the goods loop with a long mixed goods formed of Dapol and kit built wagons while 'Western' D1061 *Western Envoy* runs into the depot sidings. The layout regularly sees visiting locomotives including, on the left, a sample of Heljan's new Class 25/3 for 'O' gauge which is stabled between test runs.

VISITORS to the *Hornby Magazine* YouTube channel will be familiar with our 'O' gauge test track as it is regularly used as the backdrop for filming new releases as we put them through their paces. However, you might also have wondered where all the stock has come from and what the future holds for this project.

First we need to wind the clock back two years to the layout's initial concept. It was intended primarily as a test track to allow us to put an increasing number of new ready-to-run 7mm scale products through their paces properly. It was no good relying on a temporary circuit of track as it wasn't doing the models justice or allowing us to give readers a full understanding of how they behaved on the track. What we really needed was a proper layout where we could run up to eight carriages or a long goods behind a locomotive.

As anyone who has considered 'O' gauge will be aware, space is always a problem. We didn't have a spare location available for the new layout – though we did consider options including a suspended layout - but we did want it to be a permanent part of our test track setup so we decided to build it as a new lower level underneath our 'OO' gauge layout Topley Dale (HM Yearbook No. 5).

This was in spring 2016. The size and height of Topley Dale versus its room dictated the overall footprint of the 'O' gauge layout and, less helpfully, that it would have to be lower than we would have liked in order to pass underneath the viaduct section of the 'OO' layout. At 26in off the ground, it wasn't ideal, but it was workable as a solution for the time being.

The initial plan called for a double track main line, goods loop, diesel depot and potential for a shunting yard. The main circuit covered 10ft x 16ft with an 'L' shaped extension at one end to accommodate the diesel depot.

New home

Fast-forward 18 months to the end of 2017 and the *Hornby Magazine* test tracks were on the move to a new building giving them a better space to be maintained in. This allowed the 'OO' gauge layout to be expanded from 11ft x 10ft to 16ft x 10ft (matching the footprint of the main 'O' gauge circuit) while the 'O' gauge track was technically reduced with the loss of the original diesel depot area. Its original main line circuits remained unaltered making it straight forward to return to service.

STATISTICS	
Title:	Project 'O'
Gauge:	'O', 32mm gauge
Scale:	7mm:1ft
Length:	16ft
Width:	10ft
Track:	Peco code 124, bullhead rail
Control:	Analogue and digital
Period:	Anything goes!

On the positive side the issues of height could now be resolved. The new room allowed plenty of vertical space to allow the 'OO' gauge layout to be raised to 4ft 6in off the ground while the 'O' gauge was then lifted to 3ft above the floor making it more comfortable to operate, work on and gain access to when climbing underneath the baseboards.

Now based in its new workshop environment we were able to set about making the layout exactly what we wanted it to be – a fully functioning test track with easy access. All the original main line track transferred across to the new location, but left us pondering how the diesel depot scene could be reintroduced. Before worrying about the depot we decided »

2 A Class 31 passes the depot with the ballast train formed of Heljan 'Catfish' and 'Dogfish' four-wheel hoppers. On the right a Dapol Class 08 waits to move out of the headshunt while the depot building plays host to a Heljan Class 37 and prototype D0280 *Falcon*.

to reverse the position of the retaining wall along the junction side of the layout from the inside to the outside of the layout while also commissioning a backdrop curtain to provide a clean view at the rear of the scenic sections. Another addition was an independent set of LED strip lights for the 'O' gauge.

With these basics completed we returned to the diesel depot plot. The solution came in using the area originally intended to become a shunting yard, but it took several attempts to come up with a track plan that would work, partly because we had been stuck on the idea of incorporating a double slip into the depot plan. Once we had put that idea aside, we discovered that using a series of left and right-hand standard Peco bullhead turnouts resolved the problems and created a depot area capable of handling up to eight locomotives while also offering a siding which can be used for both analogue and digital locomotives. The remaining part of this area is permanently controlled with digital to avoid the need for section switches.

The scenic elements of the 'O' gauge layout are very much in their infancy. Being a non-exhibition layout, time to develop the railway beyond the trackwork has been limited, but there have been steps in the right direction including construction of a KS Laser Designs double track bridge to form a scenic break, the addition of a series of Intentio laser cut blind brick arches as the background on the junction side and, more recently, the start of work on the GWR Air Raid Precaution (ARP) signalbox from Intentio to stand guard over train movements. These are just the first elements around the junction as we also intend adding signals and other lineside features to bring the area to life in time.

3 'Western' D1013 *Western Ranger* passes through the junction with the passenger set of Heljan Mk 1 stock. All of the track is Peco code 124 with bullhead rail.

On the opposite side with the diesel depot scenic progress is even more basic. The track is fully laid and a Heljan diesel depot kit has been assembled as the starting point for the depot scene. However, like all the laser cut products around the junction, this needs painting, detailing and weathering to bring it to completion. Ground cover is still just a note on the job list for the future.

Operation

All the trackwork on Project 'O' is Peco code 124 with bullhead rail. The outer circuit and loops use flexible yard lengths of track throughout while the inner circuit uses Peco set track second radius curves to establish the corner profiles for the layout. These are on the limit for some locomotives – particularly large Co-Co diesels – and stock selection has to be made carefully to avoid buffer locking in some cases. That said, as a testing point the second radius curves are very useful and also allow a »

5 The pointwork adjacent to the signalbox allows trains to be reversed. In the future a second junction will be added on the opposite side of the layout at the other end of the loop to further enhance its operational flexibility. Here a Heljan Class 37 with Railtec transfers crosses into the goods loop from the inner circuit.

4 2018 has seen three new GWR steam designs arrive for 'O' including the Heljan '61XX' 2-6-2T (left) and Dapol '57XX' 0-6-0PT.

PROJECT 'O' TRACK DIAGRAM (Not to scale)

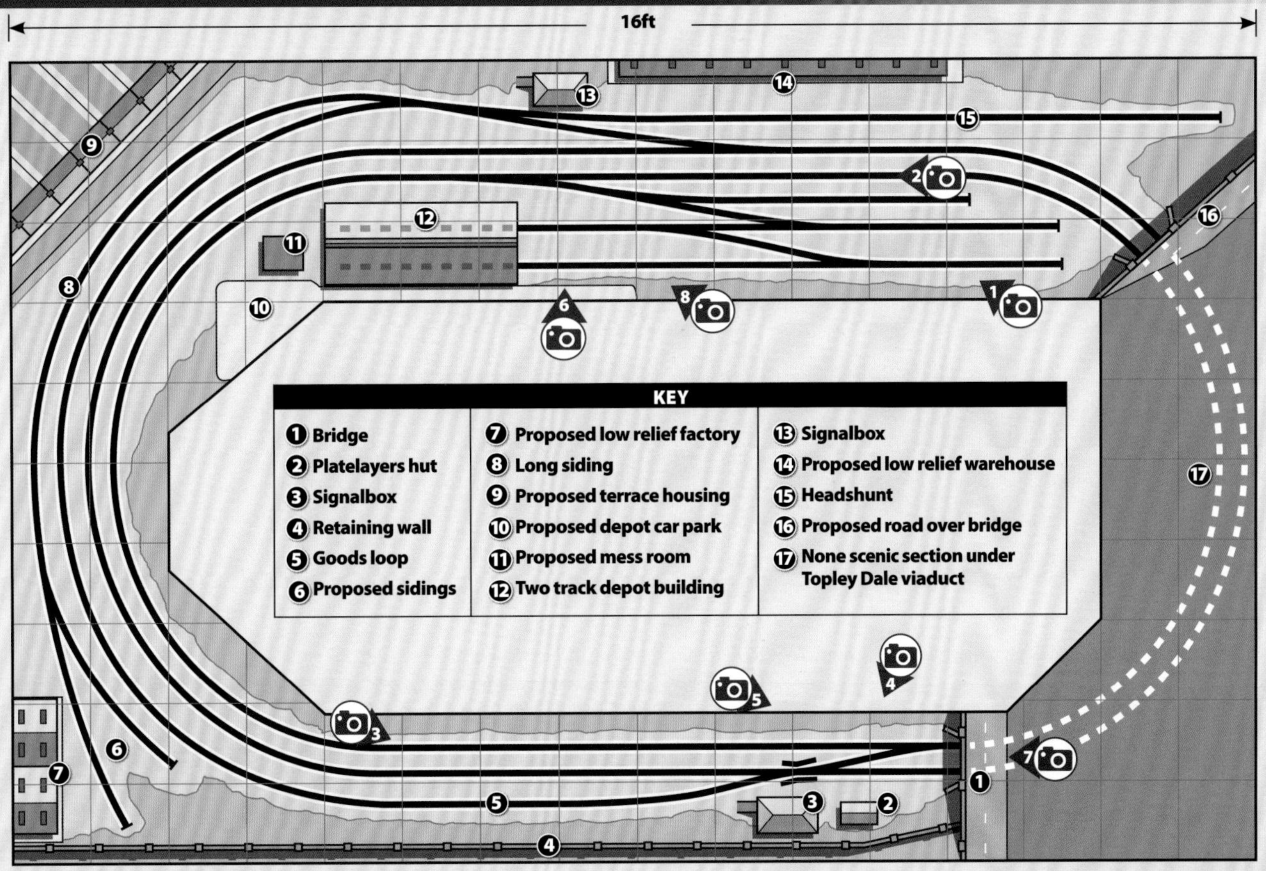
16ft
10ft
KEY
1 Bridge
2 Platelayers hut
3 Signalbox
4 Retaining wall
5 Goods loop
6 Proposed sidings
7 Proposed low relief factory
8 Long siding
9 Proposed terrace housing
10 Proposed depot car park
11 Proposed mess room
12 Two track depot building
13 Signalbox
14 Proposed low relief warehouse
15 Headshunt
16 Proposed road over bridge
17 None scenic section under Topley Dale viaduct

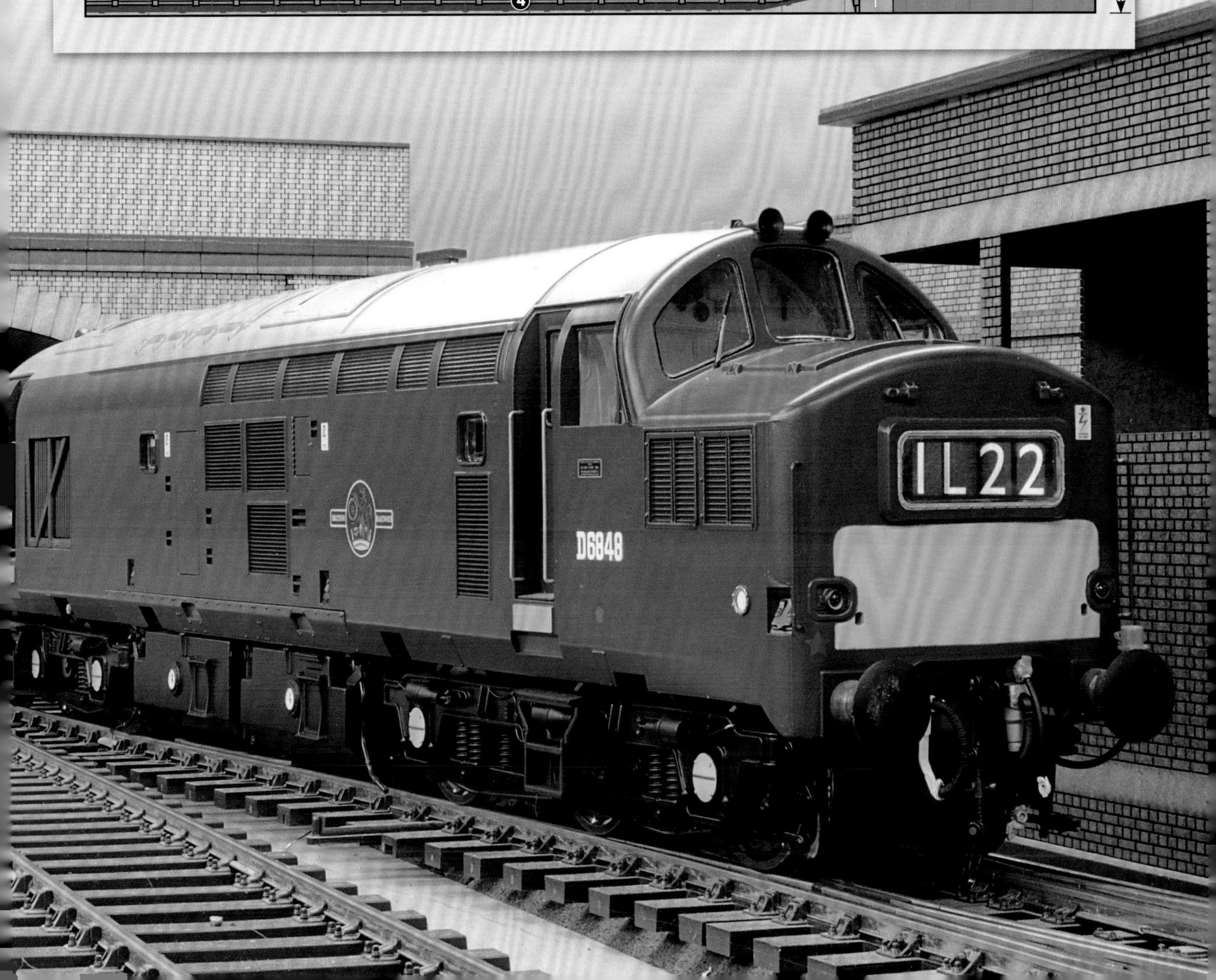
1L22
D6848

6 On shed a new Heljan Class 25/3 on test (right) stables with classes 20 and 37. The depot building is yet to be painted, weathered and detailed.

full circuit to be fitted into an 8ft 6in diameter circle.

Points consist of standard left and right turnouts with the addition of one double slip on the outer circuit to gain access to the goods loop from the inner circuit. Plans are in place to add a second double slip on the opposite side of the layout so the goods loop can become bi-directional, simplifying the exchange of trains between the two circuits.

Like the 'OO' gauge layout the 'O' gauge circuits offer dual control options. Simple plug-in terminal blocks allow Digital Command Control (DCC) or analogue controllers to be connected to the layout to drive the trains, though the inclusion of a double slip on the outer circuit means that is now DCC only. The inner however can be run with either control system and its takes around 20 seconds to switch between the two.

The 'O' gauge uses the same Gaugemaster Prodigy base station as the 'OO' gauge layout above it – trains rarely run on both at the same time, so we have had no problems with the 3.5amp capacity of the Prodigy – while analogue operation on the 'O' gauge is handled by a Helmsman 5amp system which provides plenty of power to operate the large twin motor Heljan 'O' gauge locomotives in all situations. Points are powered by DCC Concepts Cobalt IP digital motors giving consistent and reliable operation of the points in all corners of the layout. These are switched from the Gaugemaster Prodigy handsets.

Rolling stock

With its dual role as a test track and a place to run-in personally owned locomotives and rolling stock, Project 'O' can be a very busy place, particularly this year as preparations are being made for a new garden railway project in 'O' gauge to take further advantage of the scale.

The collection of locomotives and rolling stock in the background includes products from Dapol, Hatton's, Heljan and Little Loco Company. The majority of the locomotives are Heljan products including classes 05, 20, 31, 33, 37, 42, 52 and 53 plus a Dapol Class 08 shunter and GWR '57XX' 2-6-2T and a Little Loco Co Class 15. The latest addition is a Heljan GWR 'Large Prairie' 2-6-2T adding diversification to the fleet.

Passenger rolling stock is currently catered for by a rake of Heljan Mk 1 carriages while the goods rake continues to expand with ready-to-run stock from Dapol alongside kit built wagons from the Parkside Models and Slaters collections. Currently on the workbench and nearing completion are two 21-ton hoppers from Parkside (one BR and one LNER) together with a Slaters LMS 20ton brake van. Next in to the works is a Parkside Models BR 12ton 'Pipe' wagon.

A recent addition to the stock line up is a rake of Heljan 'Catfish' and 'Dogfish' ballast hoppers. Several of these have been repainted from 1970s olive green into original BR black to create an eight wagon train. All of the repaints have been painted externally with Halfords' satin black while the hopper interiors have been decorated using Railmatch BR bauxite – a close match to the factory colour used by Heljan. Transfers for these wagons are from Railtec's extensive range.

The next project for rolling stock is development of a parcels train with an Ian Kirk kit for a Gresley Corridor Full Brake waiting in the wings to join a Heljan Mk 1 BG and GUV. Future aspirations include the addition of a Southern Railway PMV van using a Slaters' kit and others to expand the parcels train further.

Future development

The 'O' gauge test track will continue to develop in time. There is no deadline for its development (which is quite refreshing!), as all of our other projects have a limited timescale to reach completion for exhibition appearances.

In the short term the plan is to build two new baseboards for one corner of the 'O' gauge layout to accommodate the return curves and storage yard of the garden railway project underneath in 2019 while we will also be looking to continue developing the scenic elements to make the railway more realistic. The second double slip will also be installed in the main lines on the depot side of the layout increasing the flexibility of operation while also ensuring that models on test have to negotiate a wider range of pointwork in different situations.

Project 'O' always has and always will be a long term project and we're looking forward to developing it further and including the latest steps in the monthly Staff Projects column as they happen. ■

USEFUL LINKS	
Dapol	www.dapol.co.uk
DCC Concepts	www.dccconcepts.com
Gaugemaster	www.gaugemaster.com
Hatton's Model Railways	www.hattons.co.uk
Heljan	www.heljan.dk
Helmsman	www.helmsmanuk.co.uk
KS Laser Designs	www.kslaserdesigns.com
Minerva Model Railways	www.minervamodelrailways.co.uk
Parkside Models	www.peco-uk.com
Peco	www.peco-uk.com
Slaters	www.slatersplastikard.com

A Heljan Class 33/0 takes the goods set back across the double slip onto the inner circuit. The bridge, buildings and retaining wall sections are all laser cut kits.

Brush prototype D0280 *Falcon* stands in the company of Class 37 D6848 and 'Warship' D869 *Zest* at the depot.

ROUTE PROFILE: WEST COAST MAIN LINE

The West Coast Main Line between London and Scotland is one of the busiest and best-known railways in the country. Throughout its history it has always been at the forefront of technological development and has carried some of our most prestigious trains. **EVAN GREEN-HUGHES** finds out why this route has become so iconic.

The West Coast Main Line included dramatic scenery and challenging gradients over the northern fells. In 1960 rebuilt 'Patriot' 4-6-0 45526 *Morecambe and Heysham* climbs Beattock near Greskine with an overnight sleeping car express from Euston with a banking engine at the rear. W.J. Verden Anderson/Rail Archive Stephenson.

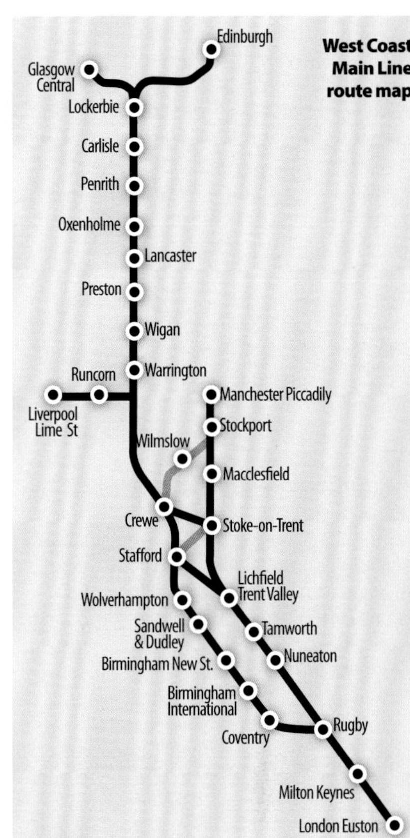

TODAY'S WEST Coast Main Line (WCML) connects some of the most important cities in Britain. Starting in London and taking in Birmingham, Liverpool, Manchester and Glasgow, this important artery has an intense service of passenger trains, not only over long distances, but also within the suburban areas that it serves. It is also one of the busiest freight routes in Europe and 40% of all the country's goods trains travel on the line at one point or another. Fully electrified on the overhead system, it can cope with trains travelling at up to 125mph.

Given the strategic nature of the line, it would be easy to fall into the trap of thinking that the whole route was conceived as one project. In fact nothing could be further from the truth. The first stretch to be completed was the Grand Junction Railway, which was the first true long-distance railway to be built in the UK. It ran from Birmingham to Newton Junction a distance of 78 miles, where it joined the Liverpool and Manchester Railway. Engineered by George Stephenson and his former pupil Joseph Locke, this railway was a fabulous success financially, largely because of contracts to carry mail which soon saw the use of dedicated mail trains with sorting facilities on board for the first time.

The impact of this route was considerable. Not only did it open up large sections of the country to travel but it also made trade in goods to and from the Americas possible to and from the West Midlands. The little village of Crewe saw the most change when in 1843 the railway moved its main workshops from Edge Hill in Liverpool to the village and what had been a sleepy little hamlet was transformed into a bustling railway town.

The route continued to develop as new sections were completed. A temporary arrangement of using a station at Vauxhall in Birmingham came to an end in 1838 when the »

London and Birmingham Railway was opened, and the two railways then shared a site at Curzon Street, a location which is soon to be reopened as part of the high speed rail network. The London and Birmingham was even longer than the Grand Junction at 112 miles and was engineered by Robert Stephenson, George's son. Commencing at a grand terminus at Euston in London, it then ran via Rugby and Coventry and onwards to Birmingham. There passengers could now merely cross the platform and continue their journey northwards. It was claimed at the time that the London and Birmingham was the greatest public work ever executed by man with the effort expended being 25% more than would have been applied in the building of the ancient pyramids.

With these two key components in place and with profit being made at a heady level, the directors of the Grand Junction could see that there could be a great future in inter-city railways. In 1840 they absorbed the Chester and Crewe Railway before it had even opened and also encouraged the development of the North Union Railway which took tracks even further north, towards Preston. The North Union was to form another essential part of what was to become the WCML and ran its first trains between Parkside, near Warrington, where it, too, made a connection with the Liverpool and Manchester, and Preston in 1838.

By the 1990s BR corporate blue schemes had given way to InterCity for express workings while carriages were now a combination of Mk 2 and Mk 3 air-conditioned stock with Driving Van Trailers at the rear. On April 13 1995 Class 87 87031 *Hal O'the Wynd* leads an up express north of Berkhamsted. Brian Stephenson.

Railway mania

Although by now the railway system was reaching out into an area which was much less populated, the so-called railway mania was now in full swing and investors queued to put their money into the new form of transport. The Lancaster and Preston Junction Railway Company was the next on the scene and it completed its line in 1840. At 20 miles long this section was one of the shortest on the eventual Anglo-Scottish route but it was one which saw much dispute in its early days as the Lancaster and Preston fell out with the North

Ex-London and North Western Railway rebuilt 'Claughton' 4-6-0s, both with Caprotti valve gear, 5908 *Alfred Fletcher* and 5962 climb Camden Bank with the 6.05pm Euston-Manchester London Road express in 1930. Double heading was frequent on the WCML in steam days, particularly with older classes, to handle the heavy loads. Frank Hebron/Rail Archive Stephenson.

'Princess Royal' 4-6-2 46210 *Lady Patricia* arrives at Manchester London Road with an express from Euston in c1955 as a 'Jubilee' departs. At this time the only overhead electrification in Manchester was for the Woodhead route 1,500v DC electrics, one of which can be seen behind the water tower. Kenneth Field/Rail Archive Stephenson.

Union, mainly over the use of Preston station.

As perhaps might have been expected traffic on this new piece of line was initially rather disappointing, particularly because the Lancaster Canal, which ran alongside the new railway, started a price war. There was also the issue of the dispute with the North Union, which resulted in the levy of a toll of 6d per passenger on the piece of track connecting the two systems and which many passengers refused to pay. In increasing difficulties, the Lancaster and Preston had no option but to lease its line to the Lancaster Canal company.

Despite the difficulties around Preston a further northwards extension was approved in 1844, this being the Lancaster and Carlisle Railway, with its mountainous route across the Shap fells. This was a massive undertaking which took no fewer than 10,000 men to complete but despite all the difficulties of the terrain the whole project was completed in two-and-a-half years. The actual route of this part of the line was hotly contested, with rival schemes being proposed running via either the Cumbrian coast or Kendal, but in the event this wild line became one of the most profitable parts of the whole scheme.

With the success of the Lancaster and Carlisle, an agreement was reached that this company would lease the Lancaster and Preston from 1846 but this decision was reversed by the shareholders with the result that confusion reigned for a while with the Lancaster and Carlisle and the Lancaster Canal Company running rival trains on the same piece of track. Two years later there was an accident when two trains collided, resulting in one death, with the cause being uncertainty as to who controlled the line. Matters were resolved in 1849 when control finally passed to the Carlisle company.

North of Carlisle tracks were provided by the Caledonian Railway which had been set up with the specific intention of providing a route from Glasgow to England. Its network reached Carlisle in 1848 when the company was only three years old, having already built lines from Edinburgh to Glasgow and then onwards over the border. By this time the various companies which had built the West Coast route south of Carlisle had been amalgamated into the London & North Western Railway (LNWR) and a simple alliance between the English and Scottish companies was formed which allowed through running on the entire route between the two capitals – the West Coast Main Line had been born.

The Premier Line

The London and North Western Railway took pride in everything that it did. Its lined black locomotives were always immaculately turned out while the punctuality of its services became legendary. For many generations such was its performance that every single General Manager was knighted and it soon gained the accolade of being the 'Premier Line' of the UK – a title it was immensely proud of.

The journey to reach that point had not been an easy one for the newly-formed company had inherited a rag-bag of assorted locomotives upon its formation in 1846: two of the constituent companies used contractor-built engines from either Sharp Brothers or Robert Stephenson while the Liverpool and Manchester used the designs of Edward Bury. The existing workshops at Crewe and Wolverton were selected for development and soon a range of basic 2-2-2 and 2-4-0 designs emerged, mainly designed by Francis Trevithick, the son of steam locomotive pioneer Richard. These were developed by James McConnell into the famous 'Bloomer' classes of 2-2-2 express engines of which 74 were built between 1851 and 1862. With their 6ft 6in or 7ft driving wheels these engines were deployed on the fastest expresses, although suffered greatly from adhesion problems due to their single driving wheels.

Perhaps the golden days of the LNWR came with the arrival of Francis Webb whose elegant 2-4-0s, particularly of the 'Precedent' class, first appeared in 1874. Although these locomotives were fairly small they could be driven very hard and subsequently were responsible for some amazing performances, particularly during the 'races to the north' which took place later in the century. One example, 790 *Hardwicke,* managed to cover 141 miles at an average speed of 67.2mph, a performance quite extraordinary for that era.

Webb's engines were improved by George Whale, whose 'Precursor' 4-4-0s and 'Experiment' 4-6-0s took engineering to another level. Further advancements came from Charles Bowen-Cooke who introduced the 'George V' 4-4-0s, which were essentially superheated 'Precursors' and which gave the southern part of the WCML a fleet of reliable fast and powerful engines.

The Caledonian, meanwhile, had also been developing its own fleet of express engines, »

LMS '8F' 2-8-0 48459 passes through Tring cutting with an up coal train in 1964. Patrick Russell/Rail Archive Stephenson

which would take over trains when they reached the new joint station which had been built in Carlisle. Like the LNWR, the Caledonian initially used 2-2-2s and 2-4-0s mainly to the design of Robert Sinclair, the line's first Chief Engineer. Following the design practice of the time, most of these locomotives had outside cylinders and many were built by outside contractors. The arrival of Dugald Drummond in 1882 saw the company building more of its own engines and the introduction of the 0-6-0 for goods work, in particular of the numerous 294 class which at one time ran to 163 examples. However, it was engineer John F. McIntosh who provided the Caledonian with some of its more outstanding designs, including the 'Dunalastair' 4-4-0s which first appeared in 1896 and four classes of 4-6-0 which were introduced for the longest and heaviest trains from 1902 onwards.

With the WCML now complete all the way from London to Glasgow, a logical step was for the LNWR and the Caledonian to come to some sort of arrangement regarding the carriages used for through services. At first a system was set up where coaches from one company would travel through to the lines of the other but then a complicated accounting exercise would take place as a result of which the owner would pay a mileage charge. This was clearly nonsensical and so in 1862 the two companies came to an agreement to provide the stock for West Coast services between them, and to form a new joint stock pool. Included in the deal were passenger vehicles, luggage vans, fish vans and Travelling Post Office vehicles, with all finished in a new livery very similar to that of the LNWR but with each vehicle bearing a new logo and lettering as 'West Coast Joint Stock'. Joint stock coaches were built to the highest standards and featured additional luggage accommodation and were always kept in the best of condition. Each coach only had a working life of around 10-20 years, after which it was taken off WCML duties and cascaded down to regular service with one or other of the owning companies.

The requirement for any form of joint working was removed when the 1923 grouping took place and both the LNWR and the Caledonian both became part of the London Midland

There were great contrasts along the 399mile route from London to Glasgow. The southern section includes surface operation of the London Underground Bakerloo Line as far as Harrow and Wealdstone. In 1939 Stanier 'Princess Royal' 4-6-2 6203 *Princess Margaret Rose* passes Bushey and Oxhey station with the down 'Royal Scot'. Rail Archive Stephenson.

& Scottish Railway (LMS). Like many other businesses, the railways were hit by the depression of that decade but Lord Stamp, the LMS chairman, was determined to see the WCML thrive.

A number of initiatives were introduced including a fast evening train from Liverpool to Euston which was booked to run the 152 miles at an average speed of just over 64mph and accelerated services on the rest of the route. While a Victorian agreement limiting overall train times between London and Scotland was observed, the LMS did steal a march on its rival, the London and North Eastern Railway (LNER), when in 1927 it ran non-stop services over the entire route using one of the new 'Royal Scot' 4-6-0s from London to Glasgow and one of the older ex-Midland 'Compound' 4-4-0s between London and Edinburgh. This was not to become a regular feature, though, due to the non-availability of corridor tenders.

The golden years

The route reached its highest profile in the years immediately before the Second World War when William Stanier introduced first his 'Princess Royal' class locomotives and later his 'Princess Coronation' 4-6-2s. The 'Coronation Scot' of 1937 was a complete streamlined train in a striking new livery which was designed to counter the publicity that the LNER was getting with its *Flying Scotsman*, something which was very effective, particularly when 6220 *Coronation* herself briefly held the world record for steam with a speed of 114mph. The new streamlined train completed its journey in 6hrs 30mins which closely matched that by the more favourable East Coast route.

London Euston has always been the southern terminus of the West Coast Main Line, but prior to electrification it sported a more traditional overall roof as well as vehicle access alongside the platforms. In 1962 two rebuilt 'Patriot' 4-6-0s have arrived: 45535 *Sir Herbert Walker K.C.B.* on the left and 45545 *Planet* on the right with the 'Ulster Express'. Patrick Russell/Rail Archive Stephenson.

In many ways these were the golden years of the West Coast route with the new family of 4-6-0s, including the 'Patriots', 'Royal Scots' and 'Jubilees' working alongside the 'Pacifics' to provide a regular fast and efficient service while at the same time goods and non-passenger traffic was exceeding all expectations. Express train speeds had risen from the average 55mph of the LNWR days and were now exceeding 60mph while doubling schemes and improvements to junctions were also assisting in reducing journey times.

The Second World War saw the line worked as it never had been before with huge troop trains and endless lines of goods wagons occupying almost every block section from the north to the south. The line became a vital artery from the ports of the west to the south and also as a supply route for those military activities that were located north of the border. Engines were worked harder than they ever had been before and maintenance of track and structures was deferred as resources were channelled towards the war effort.

The war's aftermath saw the WCML in a very run-down state and the nationalisation of the whole of the country's railway system took place. It was evident that investment would be required but this was to be some years in coming. Train working returned to a similar pattern as before the war but with express timings vastly reduced, for instance the best Glasgow-London time in the 1950s was only 7hrs 15mins, some 45mins longer than two decades previously. The railway was also losing traffic to other forms of transport, in particular domestic airlines which could offer faster times, even allowing for travel to and from airports. It became obvious that for the line to be able to compete end-to-end times would have to be reduced.

Crewe station bustles with activity in 1962 as Stanier 'Duchess' 4-6-2 46236 *City of Bradford* waits to leave with an up express. Rail Archive Stephenson.

Creating the 'buzz'

Developments in Europe had shown that electrification could achieve vastly accelerated train timings while the electrification of the Sheffield to Manchester route proved that such long-distance schemes were possible. In 1955 British Railways launched its Modernisation Plan which had at its core the conversion of most main line railways to use electric power with that power being provided by electricity generated from the use of domestically-mined coal.

The WCML was to be amongst the first to be modernised, not only by the application of electric power but also by improvements to the track, signalling, infrastructure and working practices. The 25kV overhead system was to be used, following successful implementation in France, as this cut down both the number of substations »

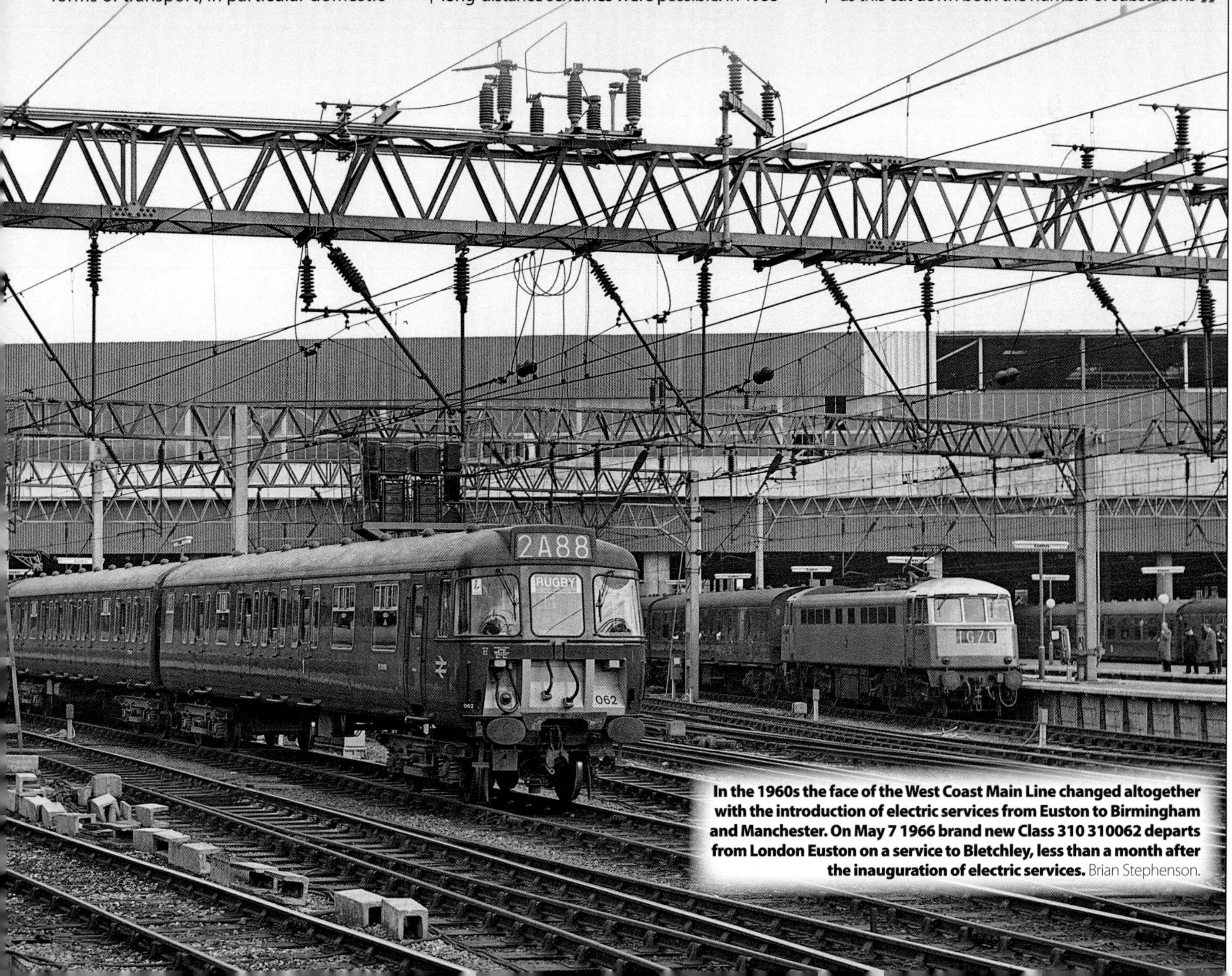

In the 1960s the face of the West Coast Main Line changed altogether with the introduction of electric services from Euston to Birmingham and Manchester. On May 7 1966 brand new Class 310 310062 departs from London Euston on a service to Bletchley, less than a month after the inauguration of electric services. Brian Stephenson.

and also the complexity of the overhead wiring. The first stretch to be completed was the Crewe to Manchester section which went live in September 1959, with a further section to Liverpool being finished three years later. By 1965 electric trains had reached London.

Electrification brought with it a series of attractive Bo-Bo locomotives which were later to become Classes 81-86. With their striking electric blue livery, these machines really did capture the public's imagination, while setting new standards for point-to-point times. London to Manchester could be achieved in 2hrs 30mins and these times were now to be offered on a regular clockface departure time system, something which was then very new. Diesels also began to be used, particularly in the transition between steam and electric, with Stanier's 'Pacifics' and 4-6-0s giving way to English Electric Type 4s and Type 3s as well as various versions of Type 2s. Suburban services were catered for by a new fleet of Electric Multiple Units which, due to their superior acceleration, reduced journey times between centres of population.

The WCML was changed forever by the modernisation of most of its principal stations. The famous Doric Arch at Euston was swept away and the site engulfed in a new station, while Birmingham, Stafford, Crewe and others all followed suit. Mercifully the grand terminus at Glasgow Central and the former interchange at Carlisle were spared.

For some years Crewe was to be the northern outpost of this modernisation and from there pairs of Class 50s took over the principal expresses, which by now were being worked by more modern Mk 2 rolling stock. Electrification, however, marched endlessly northwards and so by 1974 it had reached Glasgow, leading to the introduction of the Class 87 locomotives, which could work a train over the entire route in a time of only five hours, an improvement of 2hrs 15mins over the latter days of steam. The initiatives worked and passenger traffic over the route doubled between 1962 and 1975. The increase in passenger numbers was credited to the 'sparks effect'.

False dawns

The early 1980s saw an attempt to raise speeds on the line by the introduction of the revolutionary Advanced Passenger Train tilting train, the idea being that curves could be taken at a higher speed if tilt were employed to assist with passenger comfort. Unfortunately, as has been well documented, this train failed on a number of fronts despite reaching 162mph while on test and was prematurely marched off to the scrapyard. More conventional additions to the West Coast fleet were 50 Class 90 locomotives, which were essentially improved Class 87s, and which replaced some of the earlier classes which were by now worn out. Driving Van Trailers were also introduced to avoid having to run locomotives round at the end of each journey.

Various plans to improve and upgrade the route came and went during the 1980s and 1990s but in 1996 Virgin Trains won the franchise to provide express passenger trains, striking a deal with Railtrack for track improvements which promised 140mph running. The track upgrade plans were abandoned but not before Virgin had invested in a fleet of Class 390 tilting express EMUs, capable of working at that speed. Nevertheless, with limited upgrades and the new stock the London to Glasgow time fell even further, with most trains making the trip in 4hrs 25mins; one even did it in 3hrs 55mins, although this was for a specially-planned run.

The modern face of West Coast Main Line passenger services are the highly successful Class 390 Pendolinos operated by Virgin Trains. These were built as nine car trains, but were later expanded to 11 vehicles to increase their capacity. On August 15 2018 390107 departs Crewe for Manchester while a second Class 390 waits to follow it to the same destination. Mike Wild.

Electrification didn't just bring wires and new locomotives, it saw stations modernised too. Class 85 E3059 arrives at a newly facelifted Runcorn with a down express for Liverpool Lime Street in 1961. Rail Archive Stephenson.

The early 1900s WCML was a world away from what we have today. In 1903 a Webb LNWR 'Dreadnought' compound enters Crewe with an express from Manchester. The location isn't far from the image of the Class 390, although looking north rather than south, and shows the radical changes to the railway layout over the last 115 years. Rail Archive Stephenson.

The Class 390s have been so successful that most sets have had to be lengthened from nine to 11 coaches and each train, despite being only between 14 and 17 years old, has already covered in excess of two million miles.

The WCML is also now one of the busiest freight corridors in the country and is the major route by which goods trains travel from the Channel Tunnel to the West Midlands, North West and Scotland. Freight trains are worked by a number of different operators and types of locomotive with the go anywhere Class 66, the very powerful Class 92 electric and now the new Class 88s being the most common. At its southern end the line accommodates heavy commuter traffic generated by companies such as West Midland Trains, while in Manchester and Liverpool Northern provides most of the shorter services. ScotRail has a heavy presence around Glasgow with all the companies taking advantage of the fully electrified system to run units including Class 319s, 320s, 321s and 323s as well as the more recent Class 350s and the latest Class 385s. A relative newcomer has been TransPennine Express which currently runs its Class 350/4s from Manchester to Glasgow but which is planning to reinstate direct Liverpool-Glasgow trains when it gets its new Class 397 'Nova' stock. Their services were for some years run by three-car diesel Class 185 units.

A bright future?

Today the WCML carries more traffic than perhaps at any time in its history. More improvements, particularly to the signalling system, are on the cards and traffic levels continue to rise year on year. Although the entire line was never planned as one unit it has for more than 150 years served the important purpose of linking the major cities of the south and the north, while at the same time providing an important artery to assist with the flow of trade.

High Speed 2 will also make a difference, connecting to the main line north of Crewe and at Birmingham. With long-distance high-speed train paths released, it is unclear what the future holds – but what is known is that it will be extremely busy and maintain its status as one of the busiest mixed-use railways anywhere in the world. The West Coast Main Line is set to remain of critical importance for passengers and freight, and to Britain's economy, many decades into the future. ■

NO STATION

Many railway operations don't revolve around a station, with depots, yards and freight hubs offering much operational potential too. **MARK CHIVERS** presents a selection of track plans for 'OO' gauge without a station in sight.

WHEN DEVELOPING a model railway track plan, it is not unusual to begin by considering a station environment and working from there. However, many railway operations can be remote from stations and offer just as much, and more in some cases, operational interest on which to base your track plan. Freight locations such as oil and stone terminals, marshalling yards and depots require a considerable space and can quite often be located some distance from passenger facilities and even populated areas.

Each of the following track plans has been designed to offer plenty of operational value with a station assumed to be off-scene, which still offers the option to run passenger services alongside freight, parcels and empty stock workings to the facilities within the respective diagrams. The first three schemes are based on a 16ft x 10ft baseboard footprint, while Plan D is slightly larger at 18ft x 10ft, offering a little extra scope. With a little modification some could be reduced to 8ft in width. All have been designed for 'OO' gauge using Peco code 75 track with live frog turnouts for added electrical continuity and could also be adapted for 'N' gauge operation too.

Given their size, the schemes would suit a garage, large shed, loft or similar and could be further adapted if the space is available. Plan A has been developed to focus on container traffic with two container terminals included. Plan B was inspired by aggregates traffic, with a stone train terminal as its main focus, while Plan C is centred on a series of carriage sidings which offers some interesting route options around the wider layout. Plan D aims to represent a busy departmental yard with civil engineering traffic to the fore, with passing passenger and freight traffic adding to the variety of train movements.

Buildings and suitable rolling stock are available from the likes of Bachmann, Heljan, Hornby, Oxford Rail, Scale Model Scenery, Scalescenes and more while accessories such as signals are also plentiful such as Dapol's working semaphore examples or colour light offerings from the likes of Absolute Aspects, Berko, CR Signals, Eckon, Train-Tech and Traintronics.

As with most track plans, a certain amount of compromise is required as it's not always possible to develop a full-scale plan within the space available, however the following track plans aim to offer schemes that capture the essence of their respective subjects while also offering the ability to maintain plenty of operation and have fun too. ■

REQUIRED!

A favourite location amongst railway photographers looking for an industrial backdrop is Peak Forest in Derbyshire. Once part of the Midland Main Line from Buxton-Manchester, this route has since been truncated to serve the quarries at Peak Forest. On August 11 2006 Class 60 60500 leads an empty rake of bogie stone hoppers past on the main lines while 66078 pauses in the sidings with a rake of MEA four-wheel box wagons. Note the rugged landscape and loading facilities in the background. John Chalcraft/Railphotoprints.uk.

PLAN 1 - CONTAINER TERMINAL

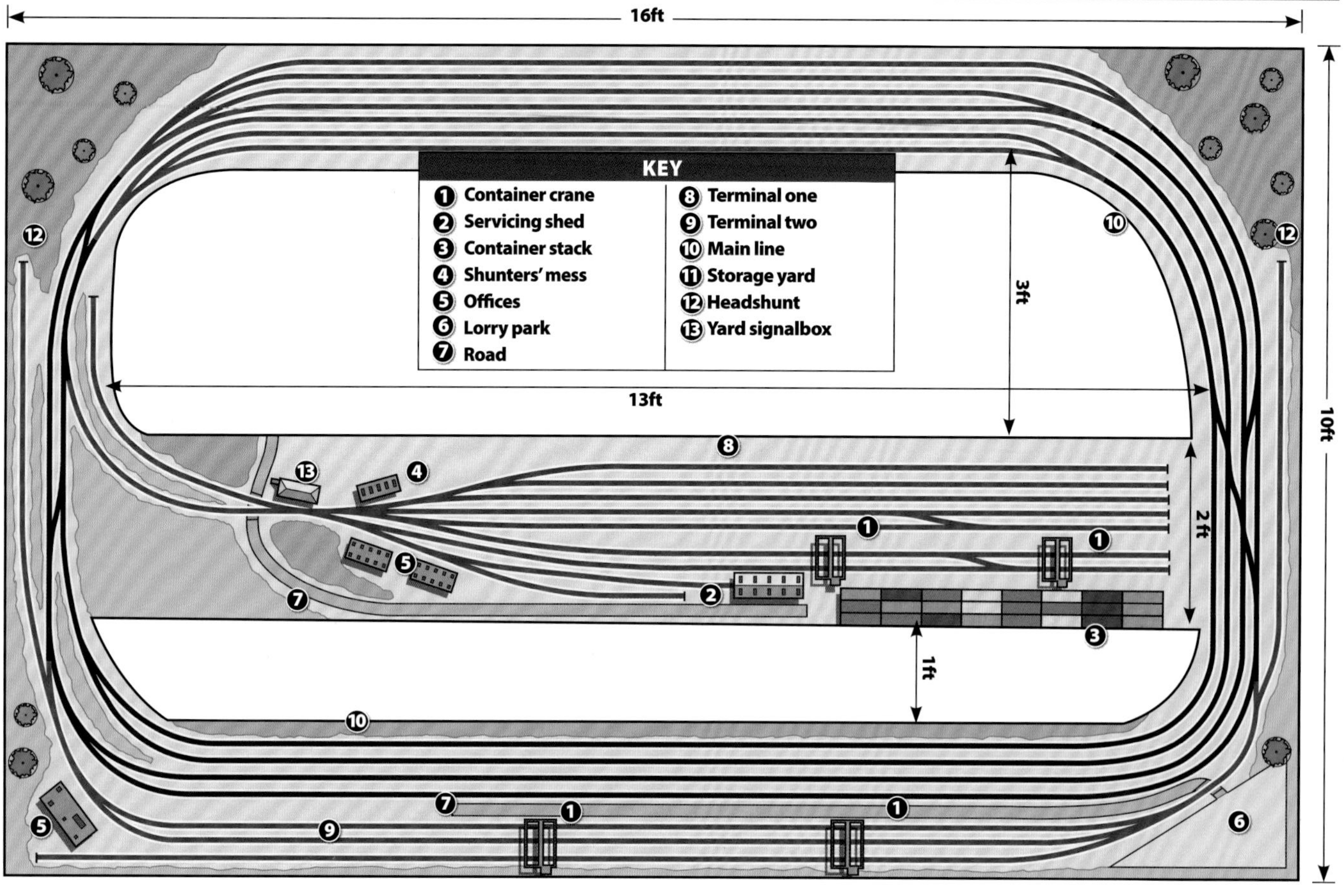

16ft | 10ft | 13ft | 3ft | 2ft | 1ft

KEY

1. Container crane
2. Servicing shed
3. Container stack
4. Shunters' mess
5. Offices
6. Lorry park
7. Road
8. Terminal one
9. Terminal two
10. Main line
11. Storage yard
12. Headshunt
13. Yard signalbox

This scheme has container traffic at the heart of its operation and features not one, but two container terminals located in the centre and lower sections of the plan, inspired very loosely by the terminals located at the Port of Southampton.

At 16ft x 10ft, the plan comprises continuous loops for the main lines, together with an additional container terminal section in the centre, with stabling sidings, run-round loops and a headshunt. This central container terminal is intended to be included as a separate 2ft wide baseboard section, which then allows access from either side in case of running issues or derailments. The lower terminal is formed of two through lines and a long single siding, for container loading/unloading operations between rail and road.

Supporting the two container terminals is a mainly four-track stretch of main line, with a short two-track section on the left-hand side of the diagram, which provides extra operational interest such as passing passenger and freight services, plus light engine movements between terminals.

Plan 1 requires 97 yards of Peco code 75 flexible track (Cat No. SL-100F) together with 39 points including curves, large, medium, double-slip and Y designs – see panel for the full component list.

Operationally, intermodal trains accessing the terminal at the centre of the plan do so through a north facing junction, with limited access to the Up and Down lines provided through turnouts to the respective storage yards at the top of the scheme. Trains to and from the lower terminal can do so from either direction, while headshunts ensure any shunting movements can be carried out without blocking the main lines. For the purposes of this scheme we have assumed two container cranes per terminal, but you could add more or even reduce this to one per terminal. Space is also included for a stack of containers within the central terminal complex and an appropriate reach stacker would be useful – Oxford Diecast produces a suitable 1:76 scale model.

A typical scenario might see a container train approach the lower terminal from the inner circuit of the two-track section on the left, cross the junction and enter the facility. It could then depart from the opposite end and negotiate the junction, crossing the four-track section to regain the inner circuit before passing through the storage yard and completing a further circuit of the layout before entering the terminal in the centre. Here, there are sidings for loading and unloading containers, together with stabling sidings, a headshunt and a locomotive servicing shed. As a result, a series of complex shunting movements could be carried out to release locomotives for servicing.

Road access to both terminals requires vehicles to cross the lines, level crossing lights (without barriers) could be added, such as those manufactured by Train-Tech (Cat No. LC10P), while containers could be stacked in the lower right-hand corner of terminal one.

Heljan made an impressive working container crane for 'OO' but this is now difficult to obtain second-hand. Bachmann has also made a static model of a container crane (Cat No. 44-0099) in its Scenecraft range as a further option.

WHAT WE USED

PRODUCT	MANUFACTURER	SCALE	CAT NO.	QUANTITY
Flexible track, yard length	Peco	'OO'	SL-100F	97
Curved double radius right point	Peco	'OO'	SL-E186	9
Curved double radius left point	Peco	'OO'	SL-E187	8
Large radius right point	Peco	'OO'	SL-E188	3
Large radius left point	Peco	'OO'	SL-E189	1
Double slip crossing	Peco	'OO'	SL-E190	3
Medium radius right point	Peco	'OO'	SL-E195	9
Medium radius left point	Peco	'OO'	SL-E196	4
Small radius 'Y' turnout	Peco	'OO'	SL-E197	1
Three-way medium radius point	Peco	'OO'	SL-E199	1

Above: **Freightliner Class 66/5 66505 shunts container wagons at Southampton Maritime terminal on May 28 2003.** John Chalcraft/Railphotoprints.uk.

PLAN 2 - STONE TERMINAL

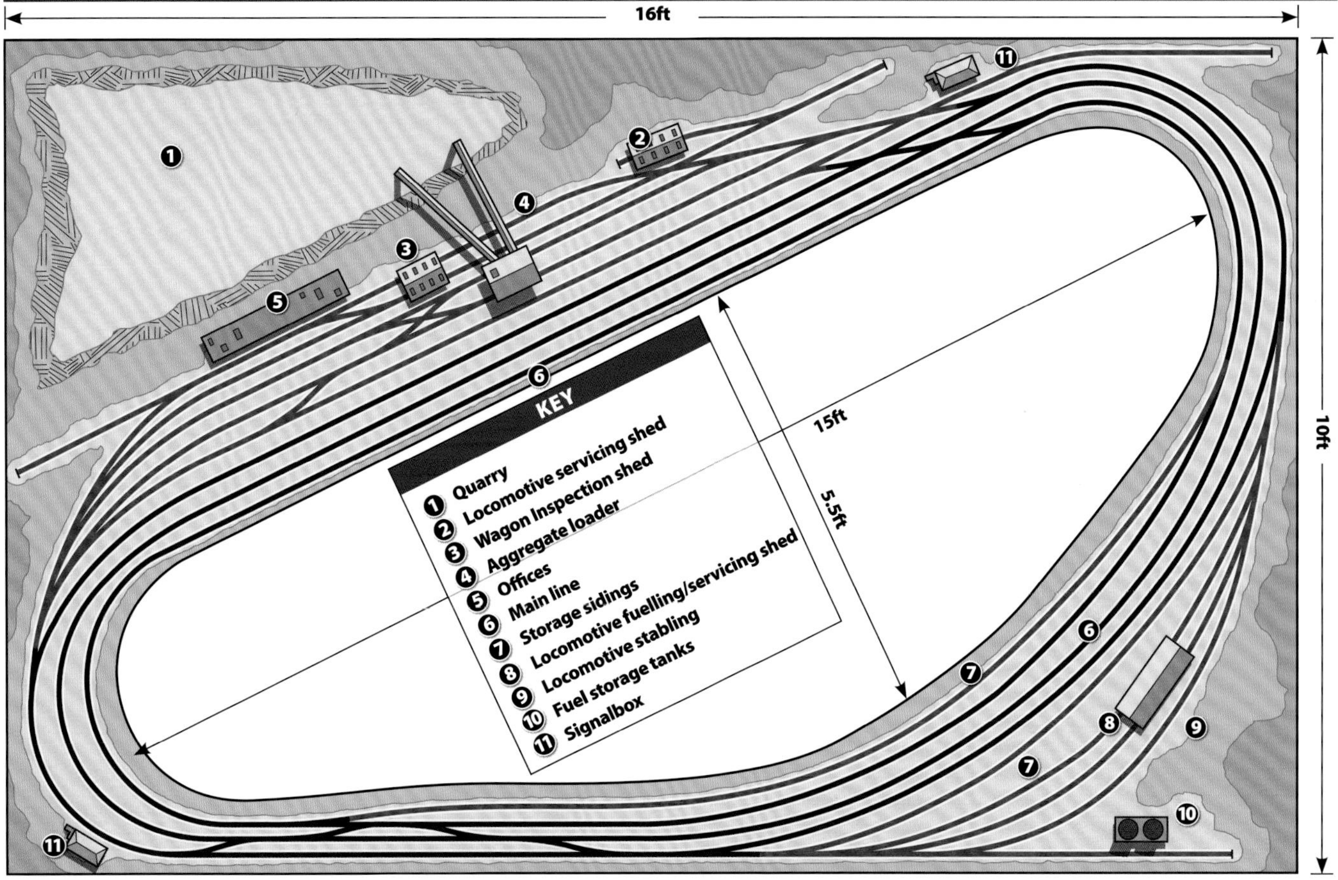

16ft | 10ft | 15ft | 5.5ft

KEY

1. Quarry
2. Locomotive servicing shed
3. Wagon Inspection shed
4. Aggregate loader
5. Offices
6. Main line
7. Storage sidings
8. Locomotive fuelling/servicing shed
9. Locomotive stabling
10. Fuel storage tanks
11. Signalbox

Plan 2 represents a rail-connected stone terminal, receiving empty wagons and despatching loaded trains as well as servicing empty vehicles between workings, along with the locomotives.

The stone terminal sidings in the upper section of the scheme provide the main focus, inspired by the terminal adjacent to the Midland Main Line at Barrow-on-Soar in Leicestershire. Highlights include a pair of lines providing access to the loading facility with a scissors-style crossing offering additional route options to and from this area, while there are also wagon and locomotive servicing sheds and a headshunt at the top of the scheme to aid train marshalling without fouling the main lines.

At 16ft x 10ft, the plan also includes a modest Traction Maintenance Depot (TMD) to the lower right for servicing and refuelling locomotives, offering additional operation for light engine movements. The main running lines are made up of three continuous loops – a Down relief line, Down main and Up main. The Down relief is intended for most of the arriving empty aggregate trains to the left of the plan, while Up services can access the terminal through the crossing at the top of the scheme. Loaded trains can depart in either direction too, although a short run of wrong-line running will be required in the lower left-hand section of the diagram to gain the crossing from the Down relief to Up main lines.

In terms of track required, the layout utilises 65 yards of Peco 'OO' gauge code 75 flexible track and 42 points ranging from medium and large straight points to curved turnouts, a trio of double-slips and a short crossing – see panel for the full component list.

WHAT WE USED

PRODUCT	MANUFACTURER	SCALE	CAT NO.	QUANTITY
Flexible track, yard length	Peco	'OO'	SL-100F	65
Curved double radius right point	Peco	'OO'	SL-E186	6
Large radius right point	Peco	'OO'	SL-E188	1
Large radius left point	Peco	'OO'	SL-E189	1
Double slip crossing	Peco	'OO'	SL-E190	3
Short crossing	Peco	'OO'	SL-E193	1
Long crossing	Peco	'OO'	SL-E194	1
Medium radius right point	Peco	'OO'	SL-E195	15
Medium radius left point	Peco	'OO'	SL-E196	16

Adams 'O2' 0-4-4T 30199 shunts a rake of ballast hoppers headed by a 'Shark' ballast plough at Meldon Quarry on August 3 1960. Dave Cobbe/Railphotoprints.uk.

Although most traffic is assumed to be formed of aggregates and ballast workings, the main lines can also be used for passenger trains. Two storage sidings have been included to accommodate some of these – one on the outer loop and another on the inner loop. Additional storage lines could be added, while locomotives can be stabled at the small TMD in the lower right-hand section of the scheme with two servicing/fuelling roads. Fuel tank wagons could also be tripped to and from the storage tank siding for further operational interest. Incidentally, a modest locomotive servicing shed is also incorporated within the stone terminal scheme, as is a wagon servicing shed.

Bachmann and Hornby include a few structures within their respective resin-cast ready-to-plant ranges that could be incorporated within the stone terminal, while Walthers 'HO' scale Valley Cement plant kit (933-3098) could perhaps be adapted to suit. With a wide selection of suitable rolling stock ranging from steam-era mineral wagons to contemporary bogie hopper wagons from the likes of Accurascale, Bachmann, Dapol, Heljan, Hornby and more, this plan could be backdated to the steam-era or adapted to suit modern day operations just as easily.

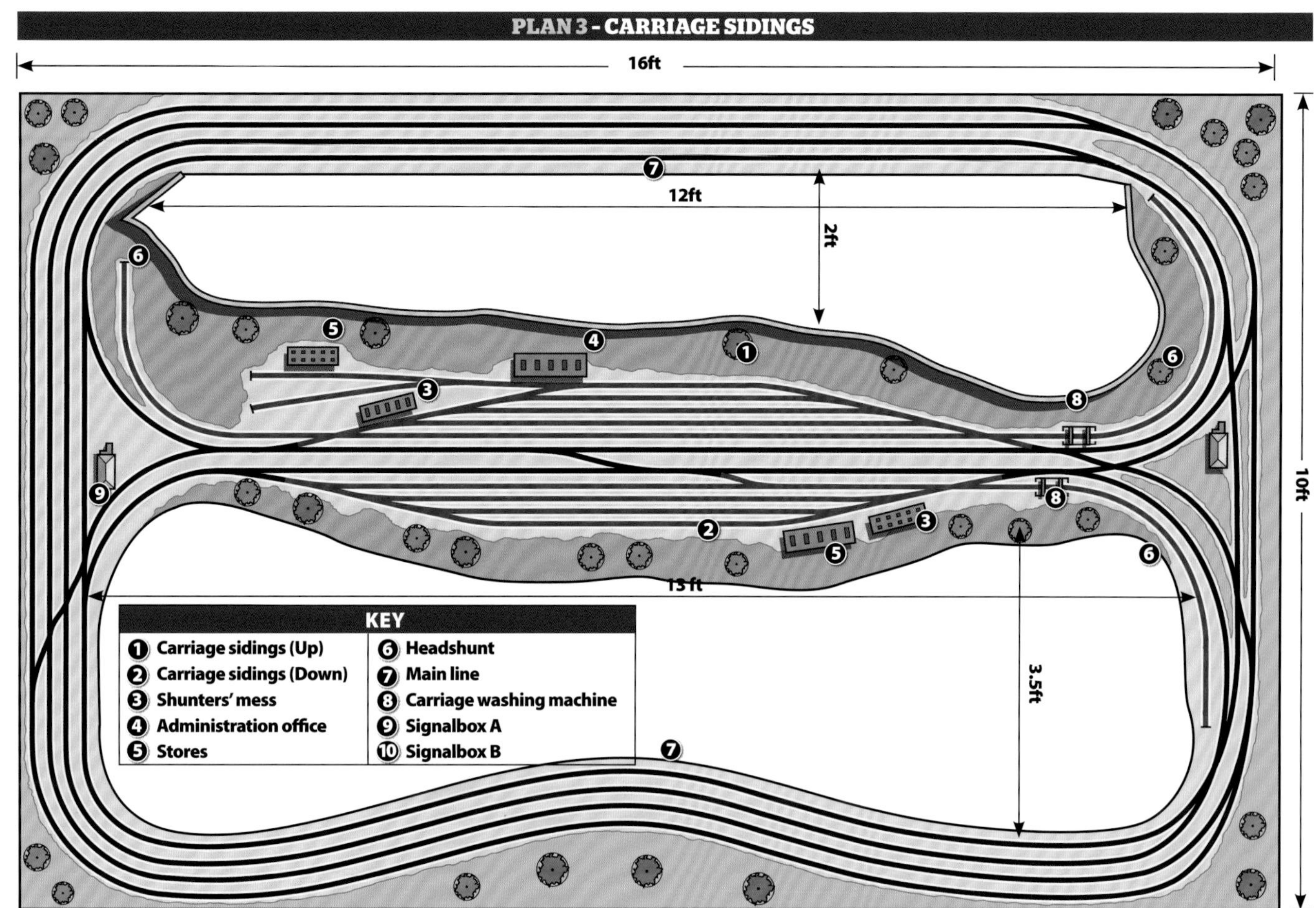

For sheer operational fun, this scheme offers plenty to keep the operator busy with a series of continuous loop circuits and a fan of carriage sidings in the centre.

While the layout features large continuous circuits, these are split into an upper and lower circuit feeding in and out of the carriage sidings. As a result, access here introduces quite complex routes between the Up and Down sidings at the centre. Much of the main plan is four-track, reducing to two at the right-hand side of the scheme, with a junction linking to/from both main running lines and the carriage sidings for maximum flexibility. Access from the outer circuit to the carriage sidings at the left of the scheme is through a junction across the four-track main line, with a simpler connection from the sidings to the inner circuit at this point.

The longest carriage sidings can easily accommodate a six-car train, while space in the remaining sidings diminishes accordingly, plus headshunts are included to save marshalling movements fouling the main lines. The Up carriage sidings include two short sidings which are intended for the yard shunting locomotive or spare carriages, together with a carriage washer at the opposite end of the yard.

At 16ft x 10ft, this plan utilises 84 yards of Peco 'OO' code 75 flexible track (SL-100F) and 31 points and crossings consisting of medium and large radius points, diamond crossings, double slips, and Y format turnouts – see panel for the full list.

Careful consideration will be required when planning the wiring for this design to ensure you address any potential polarity issues. However, this scheme offers plenty of main line running, with multiple routes to choose from, as well as marshalling carriages within the sidings. For example, a train setting out from the Up carriage sidings could head through the junction to the right of the scheme and join the main lines to the lower section of the scheme, keeping to the full extent of the outer slow line, before negotiating the junction at the right of the diagram to enable access to the Down carriage sidings. Alternatively, you could bypass the sidings on this occasion and complete a circuit of the lower half of the layout, before entering the Down carriage sidings. As the fast lines on the four-track section cannot access the junction for the carriage sidings, additional circuits could be factored in too.

WHAT WE USED

PRODUCT	MANUFACTURER	SCALE	CAT NO.	QUANTITY
Flexible track, yard length	Peco	'OO'	SL-100F	84
Curved double radius right point	Peco	'OO'	SL-E186	4
Curved double radius left point	Peco	'OO'	SL-E187	5
Large radius right point	Peco	'OO'	SL-E188	4
Double slip crossing	Peco	'OO'	SL-E190	4
Short crossing	Peco	'OO'	SL-E193	5
Long crossing	Peco	'OO'	SL-E194	1
Medium radius right point	Peco	'OO'	SL-E195	8
Medium radius left point	Peco	'OO'	SL-E196	10
Small radius 'Y' turnout	Peco	'OO'	SL-E197	2

Left: **Class 09 09005 shunts the carriage sidings at Clapham Junction in the company of 4-VEP 7417 and Class 73 electro-diesel 73105 on June 14 1985.** Gordon Edgar/Railphotoprints.uk.

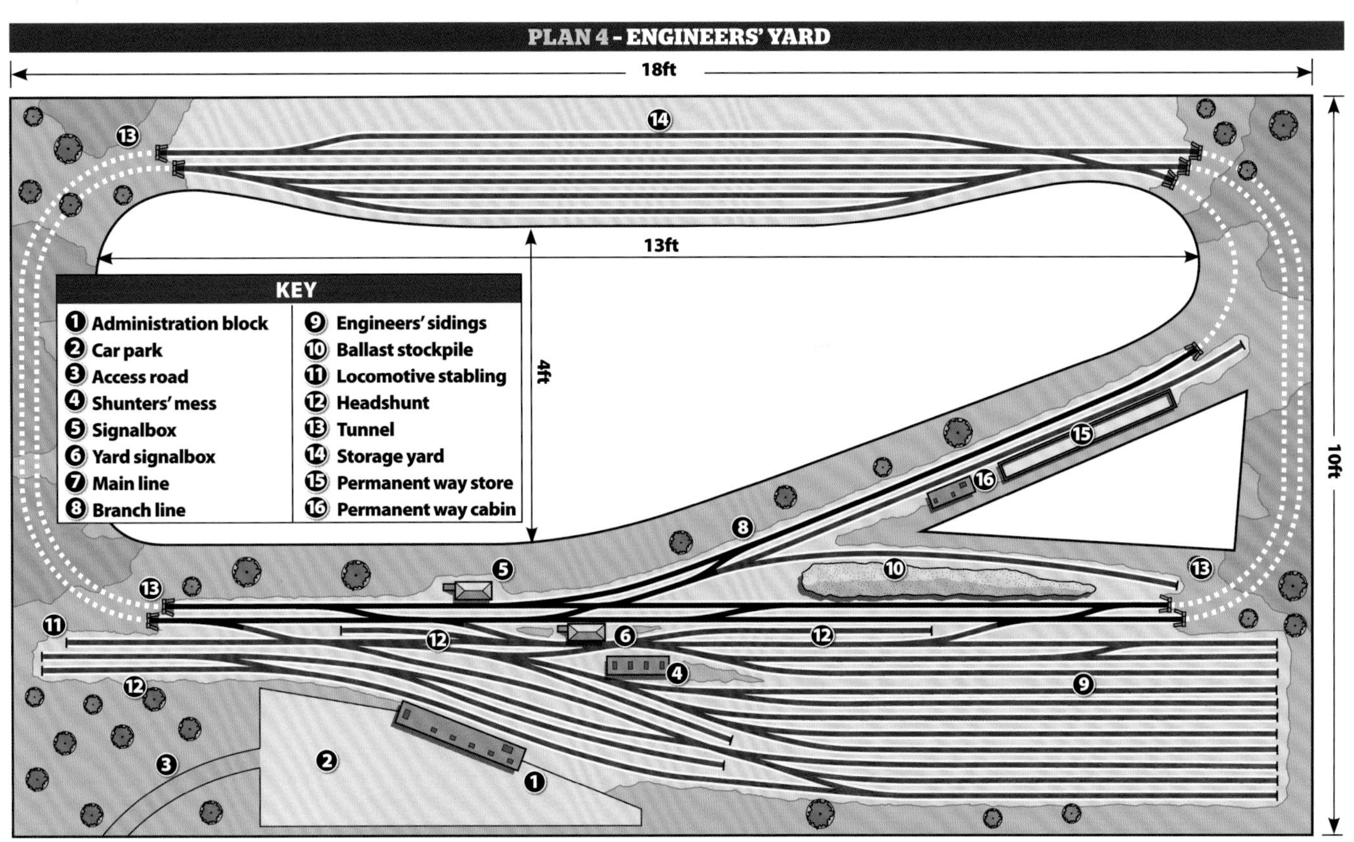

Plan D represents a busy civil engineers' yard and offers plenty of scope for shunting operations as well as main line running too.

Inspired by the yard at Hoo Junction in Kent, this scheme features sidings, run-round loops, headshunts and locomotive stabling points to keep the operator busy, plus there are also a couple of sidings opposite the main yard for loading permanent way materials.

At 18ft x 10ft the plan is a little larger than the previous schemes and is very track intensive, requiring 88 yards of Peco 'OO' code 75 flexible track (SL-100F) and 45 points and crossings – see panel for the full component list.

Focusing on the main yard area in the lower section of the scheme, trains enter and exit from the adjacent two-track main line of the continuous loop circuit. Towards the centre, a single-line branch diverges from the main line and links back into the main circuits within the storage yard area at the top. Tunnel sections help to reduce the visual impact of the curves in the scenic sections. The yard has two entry points and three exits, while headshunts and loops provide the flexibility for shunt releasing trains using yard shunters and also offer the scope for train marshalling to take place. The scheme is large enough that multiple shunting movements could be undertaken at the same time. Empty ballast or materials wagons could also be tripped from the main yard to one of the sidings towards the centre of the plan. These could exit the main yard from the centre of the scheme and propel back through the single slip junction, gaining access to the appropriate siding.

The single line branch is controlled from the signalbox and features a short double-track section with a useful single slip at the junction with the main line. This line could see other forms of freight traffic or passenger trains for added variety. Six storage sidings are included at the top of the plan for further trains, including passenger formations, with tunnels separating this area and the main scenic section.

You could operate the layout from the centre, while a limited access space is included to the lower right-hand side of the plan in case you need to reach through and access any potential derailments in this corner of the layout, as it could be difficult to lean across otherwise. For the best access this layout could be developed as an exhibition scheme.

For rolling stock, Bachmann, Hornby, Dapol, Heljan, Kernow Model Rail Centre and more offer a wide selection of departmental wagons that would be suitable for use. Plastic kits from the Cambrian and Parkside ranges are also available, while for something a little different, Make Your Mark Models produces a useful Plasser and Theurer 12ton engineering rail-mounted crane (HM101).

WHAT WE USED

PRODUCT	MANUFACTURER	SCALE	CAT NO.	QUANTITY
Flexible track, yard length	Peco	'OO'	SL-100F	88
Single slip crossing	Peco	'OO'	SL-E180	1
Double slip crossing	Peco	'OO'	SL-E190	3
Medium radius right point	Peco	'OO'	SL-E195	16
Medium radius left point	Peco	'OO'	SL-E196	22
Small radius 'Y' turnout	Peco	'OO'	SL-E197	1
Large radius 'Y' turnout	Peco	'OO'	SL-E198	1
Three-way medium radius point	Peco	'OO'	SL-E199	1

Above: **Class 33/0 33008 *Eastleigh* double heads with Class 33/1 33116 near Fairwood Junction with a Tonbridge-Meldon Quarry empty ballast working on November 23 1989.** John Chalcraft/Railphotoprints.uk.

USEFUL LINKS

Absolute Aspects	*www.absoluteaspects.com*
Accurascale	*www.accurascale.co.uk*
Bachmann	*www.bachmann.co.uk*
Berko/Eckon	*www.onlinemodelsltd.co.uk*
CR Signals	*www.crsignals.com*
Dapol	*www.dapol.co.uk*
Heljan	*www.heljan.dk*
Hornby	*www.hornby.com*
Kernow Model Rail Centre	*www.kernowmodelrailcentre.com*
Make Your Mark Models	*www.makeyourmarkmodels.com*
Metcalfe Models	*www.metcalfemodels.com*
Oxford Rail	*www.oxfordrail.com*
Peco	*www.peco-uk.com*
Scale Model Scenery	*www.scalemodelscenery.co.uk*
Scalescenes	*www.scalescenes.com*
Train-Tech	*www.train-tech.com*
Traintronics	*www.traintronics.co.uk*

WEST COAST MAIN LINE

Passenger workings 1960-2010

The West Coast Main Line boasts a long tradition of sleek, powerful trains, many of which can be replicated in model form from ready-to-run rolling stock, as **MARK CHIVERS** explains.

AT JUST SHY OF 400 miles long, the West Coast Main Line (WCML) has seen its fair share of variety when it comes to motive power and rolling stock. Linking London with Birmingham, North West England and Scotland it was built in stages from the mid-1830s. It serves significant populations including Birmingham, Carlisle, Crewe, Glasgow, Liverpool, Manchester, Northampton, Preston, Stafford, Stoke-on-Trent, Warrington, Wigan and Wolverhampton.

By the 1960s British Railways' plans to modernise had brought about a transition from steam to diesel and electric operation with a mix of traction at the time that included Stanier 'Princess Coronation' 4-6-2s, rebuilt 'Royal Scot' 4-6-0s, BR 'Britannia' 4-6-2s, English Electric Prototype DP2, English Electric Type 4 (Class 40) diesels and more at the head of express and named workings. With a phased introduction of electrification, this resulted in some quite interesting workings with steam and diesel-hauled services operating side-by-side for a spell, with electric locomotives progressively taking over as electrification was extended. From the late 1960s Class 50 locomotives appeared on services north of Crewe, until this too was electrified during the first half of the 1970s. A full electric timetable was introduced in 1974.

Since then a succession of AC electric locomotives have plied the WCML out of London Euston including classes 81-87 and 90 on passenger services, many of which could run to a dozen or more carriages. Even in the 1960s named trains could be long affairs with up to 15 vehicles possible on services such as the 'Mid-Day Scot' between London Euston and Glasgow Central and other grandly titled trains including the 'Caledonian' (Glasgow Central to Euston), the 'Northern Irishman' (Euston to Stranraer), the 'Red Rose' (Euston to Liverpool Lime Street), the 'Royal Scot' (Euston to Glasgow Central), the 'Ulster Express' (Euston to Heysham) and more.

In later years the number of named trains reduced under British Rail, but standout services included the 'Manchester Pullman', with its unique set of dedicated Mk 2 Pullman cars, and the BR Mk 3 Pullman services to/from Liverpool and Manchester. BR's Motorail and overnight 'Sleeper' operations were also quite lengthy affairs, one of which regularly included a BR Mk 1 Pullman Bar Car in its formation. Even today's Caledonian Sleeper service remains the longest passenger train to use London Euston, formed of 16 carriages.

Long-distance WCML present-day duties are predominantly in the hands of Virgin Trains' Class 390 Pendolinos (plus a handful of Class 221 Super Voyagers) supplemented by London and North Western Railway Class 319 or Class 350 Desiro Electric Multiple Units (EMUs) on stopping services to/from London Euston, with further variety on services emanating from population hotspots along the line - plus, of course freight.

Modellers of the post-1960 WCML scene have been reasonably well catered for with a good selection of 'OO' steam and diesel prototypes covered, plus a growing roster of suitable AC electric models. New and recent additions include Hornby's newly-tooled 'OO' gauge Stanier 'Princess Coronation' 4-6-2 and BR Class 87 Bo-Bo electric locomotive, together with new rolling stock such as Bachmann's 'OO' gauge BR Mk 1 Carflat wagons and BR Mk 2f Open First (FO), Restaurant First Buffet/Open (RFB/RFO), Tourist Open Standard (TSO) and Brake Open Standard (BSO) coaches, Hornby's BR Mk 1 FO and BSO carriages, Oxford Rail's 57ft BR Motorail Carflat wagons and BR Mk 3a locomotive-hauled FO, TSO and Restaurant/Buffet (RFM/RUB) carriages.

Tri-ang/Hornby first dabbled with overhead electrics in the late 1950s/early 1960s, advertising its 'OO' gauge overhead power supply system (or catenary) in connection with its EM2 1,500V DC Co-Co electric. In 1966 an AL1 (Class 81) Bo-Bo AC electric locomotive was added, but it wasn't until 1981 that the next AC electric appeared from the manufacturer in the form of the Class 86, which has appeared in a wide variety of colour schemes since. This was followed by the Class 90 in the late 1980s. In 1995, Hornby's Class 92 Co-Co was added to the range. Lima added the Class 87 Bo-Bo electric to its range of

VEHICLE DESIGNATIONS	
BG	Gangwayed Brake
BCK	Corridor Brake Composite
BFK	Corridor Brake First
BSK	Corridor Brake Second/Standard
CK	Corridor Composite
FK	Corridor First
FO	Open First
GUV	General Utility Van
RB	Restaurant Buffet
RBK	Restaurant Kitchen Buffet
RBR	Restaurant Buffet Refurbished
RFM	Restaurant First Modular
RFO	Restaurant First Open
RMB	Restaurant Miniature Buffet
RU	Restaurant Unclassified
RUB	Restaurant Unclassified Buffet
SK	Corridor Second/Standard
SLC	Sleeper Composite
SLE	Sleeper Either Class
SLEP	Sleeper Either Class with Pantry
SLF	Sleeper First
SLS	Sleeper Second/Standard
SLSTP	Sleeper Second/Standard Twin Berth with Pantry
SO	Open Second/Standard
TSO	Tourist Open Second/Standard

USEFUL LINKS	
Bachmann	*www.bachmann.co.uk*
Dapol	*www.dapol.co.uk*
Heljan	*www.heljan.dk*
Hornby	*www.hornby.com*
Invicta Model Rail	*www.invictamodelrail.com*
Kernow Model Rail Centre	*www.kernowmodelrailcentre.com*
Oxford Rail	*www.oxfordrail.com*
Replica Railways	*www.replicarailways.co.uk*
Southern Pride Models	*www.southernpridemodels.co.uk*

'OO' gauge models in the late 1970s, the tools of which were absorbed into the Hornby range some years later, along with its interpretation of the Class 92. Heljan's Class 86 Bo-Bo electric was announced in 2010, with five liveries initially including BR heritage blue, InterCity and Virgin Trains colours. To date, no further models of the Heljan Class 86 have been produced though Heljan has confirmed that it will be producing the Class 86/0 in the future for 'OO'.

Meanwhile, Bachmann's first AC electric model – the Class 85 Bo-Bo – was unveiled in 2012, while its most recent AC electric locomotive, the Class 90, is nearing release with completed models expected in March 2019. Further signature modern-era traction includes Hornby's 'OO' gauge Class 390 in Virgin Trains (VT) colours and Bachmann's Silverlink/London Midland Class 350 Desiro EMUs, plus Bachmann's VT Class 220 Voyager and Class 221 Super-Voyager models.

Hornby's Period III Stanier coaches are suitable for use within WCML formations in the 1960s with Corridor First (FK), Corridor Second (SK) and Brake Corridor Second (BSK) variants available, although the lack of a Corridor Composite (CK) in the range will require the use of Dapol's older-tooled model. BR Mk 1 coaches are well represented between the Bachmann and Hornby ranges, covering daytime and night-time possibilities thanks to the former's BR Mk 1 Sleeper First (SLF) and Sleeper Standard Twin Berth with Pantry (SLSTP) sleeper vehicles and more. Bachmann's Mk 2 range offers a good selection of vehicle types in blue/grey, while Hornby's BR Mk 2e vehicles are offered in BR blue/grey, InterCity 'swallow' and Virgin Trains colour schemes. Bachmann's new BR Mk 2f vehicles will appear initially in BR blue/grey and BR InterCity liveries while Oxford Rail's new BR Mk 3a carriages are now available in BR InterCity 'Swallow' and BR blue/grey liveries, with Virgin Trains examples also planned.

As much as we'd love to model full length express trains in 'OO', it is not always possible given space constraints. The following selection of passenger train formations represents a brief glimpse of WCML operations over a 50-year period with some selective compression. With a little modellers licence, some interesting and impressive WCML formations can be achieved using off the shelf products. ■

SUITABLE 'OO' GAUGE PASSENGER COACHING STOCK

TYPE	COLOUR SCHEME	MANUFACTURER	CAT NO.
SR PMV	BR green	Bachmann	39-530
SR Bogie Van B	BR green	Hornby	R4536
LMS 57ft Carflat	BR Motorail blue	Oxford Rail	OR76CAR003B
Stanier PIII CK	BR maroon	Dapol	4P-010-033
Stanier PIII SK	BR maroon	Hornby	R4235C
Stanier PIII FK	BR maroon	Hornby	R4234B
Stanier PIII BSK	BR maroon	Hornby	R4236C
BR Mk 1 BG	BR blue/grey	Bachmann	39-175E
BR Mk 1 BG	BR blue/grey	Hornby	R4646
BR Mk 1 BG	BR maroon	Bachmann	39-176F
BR Mk 1 BG	BR maroon	Hornby	R4625
BR Mk 1 BCK	BR blue/grey	Bachmann	39-225C
BR Mk 1 BSK	BR maroon	Bachmann	39-076G
BR Mk 1 BSK	BR maroon	Hornby	R4352
BR Mk 1 BSK	BR blue/grey	Bachmann	39-075D
BR Mk 1 BSO	BR maroon	Hornby	R4788
BR Mk 1 BSO	BR blue/grey	Hornby	R4777
BR Mk 1 BSP	*Nightcap Bar* BR blue/grey	Bachmann	39-321
BR Mk 1 CCT	BR blue	Bachmann/Invicta Model Rail	39-551Z
BR Mk 1 CK	BR maroon	Bachmann	39-126F
BR Mk 1 CK	BR maroon	Hornby	R4350
BR Mk 1 CK	BR blue/grey	Bachmann	39-125C
BR Mk 1 FK	BR blue/grey	Bachmann	39-150C
BR Mk 1 FO	BR maroon	Hornby	R4789
BR Mk 1 FO	BR blue/grey	Hornby	R4778
BR Mk 1 GUV	BR blue/grey	Bachmann	39-274
BR Mk 1 GUV	BR InterCity	Bachmann	39-276
BR Mk 1 GUV	BR InterCity	Hornby	R6354
BR Mk 1 GUV	BR blue	Bachmann	39-277
BR Mk 1 POS	BR blue/grey	Bachmann	39-425
BR Mk 1 RMB	BR blue/grey	Bachmann	39-264
BR Mk 1 RB	BR blue/grey	Bachmann	39-100C
BR Mk 1 RBR	BR blue/grey	Mainline	37-113
BR Mk 1 RBR	BR InterCity	Bachmann	39-104
BR Mk 1 RU	BR maroon	Bachmann	39-103C
BR Mk 1 SK	BR maroon	Bachmann	39-026H
BR Mk 1 SK	BR maroon	Hornby	R4351
BR Mk 1 SLF	BR maroon	Bachmann	39-500
BR Mk 1 SLSTP	BR maroon	Bachmann	39-502A
BR Mk 1 SLF	BR blue/grey	Bachmann	39-501
BR Mk 1 SLSTP	BR blue/grey	Bachmann	39-503A
BR Mk 1 TSO	BR blue/grey	Bachmann	39-050F
BR Mk 1 TSO	BR NSE	Bachmann	39-058
BR Mk 1 Carflat	BR Motorail blue	Bachmann	38-902

The West Coast Main Line was the stamping ground for a long list of high profile locomotives including Stanier's 'Duchess' 4-6-2s, the English Electric Class 40s and, from the mid 1970s, the Class 87 'Electric Scots'. Representing the early years of the class, Hornby's 2018 model of 87035 *Robert Burns* passes West Coast Cement works with a mixed rake of Mk 1 and Mk 2 stock.

Stanier 'Black Five' 4-6-0 BR black (Hornby), BR Mk 1 BSK, SK, SK, SLSTP, SLF, CK, SK, BSK, BG – BR maroon
DATE: 1961 **SERVICE:** 'The Northern Irishman' (Euston-Stranraer) **LOCATION:** Carlisle

BR Standard '8P' 4-6-2 BR lined green, late crests (Hornby), Stanier CK, BSK, SK – BR maroon
DATE: 1962 **SERVICE:** Euston-Crewe **LOCATION:** Rugby

Stanier 'Princess Coronation' 4-6-2 BR lined maroon, late crests (Hornby), BR Mk 1 BCK, CK, SK, BSK, BSK, SO, RK, FK, BSK – BR maroon
DATE: 1962 **SERVICE:** Euston-Perth **LOCATION:** Carlisle

Stanier 'Princess Coronation' 4-6-2 BR lined maroon, late crests (Hornby), BR Mk 1 BSK, SK, SO, SO, RKB, FO, FK, BSK – BR maroon
DATE: 1962 **SERVICE:** Euston-Glasgow Central **LOCATION:** Carlisle

Class 40 BR green (Bachmann/Hornby), BR Mk 1 BSK, SK, SO, SO, RK, FO, FK, CK, BSK – BR maroon
DATE: 1962 **SERVICE:** 'The Red Rose' (Euston-Liverpool) **LOCATION:** Crewe

Class 85 BR blue with white cab roof (Bachmann), Stanier Period III SK, BSK, BR Mk 1 FK, FO, RKB, SO, CK, Stanier Period III SK, BR Mk 1 BSK – BR maroon
DATE: 1962 **SERVICE:** Liverpool Lime Street-Euston **LOCATION:** Wallerscote

English Electric DP2 BR green (Heljan), BR Mk 1 BSK, Stanier Period III SK, BR Mk 1 SO, RKB, FO, SO, FK, BSK – BR maroon
DATE: 1963 **SERVICE:** Euston-Perth **LOCATION:** Lancaster

Rebuilt 'Royal Scot' 4-6-0 BR lined green, late crests (Hornby), Stanier Period III BSK, SK, BSK – BR maroon
DATE: 1963 **SERVICE:** Carlisle-Glasgow Central **LOCATION:** Beattock

Class 40 BR green (Bachmann/Hornby), BR Mk 1 BSK, SK, SK, SK, SO, RKB, FO, FK, BFK
DATE: 1963 **SERVICE:** 'The Caledonian' (Euston to Glasgow) **LOCATION:** Weaver Junction

BR 'Clan' 4-6-2 BR lined green, late crests (Hornby), BR Mk 1 BSK, CK, SK, BSK, BG, Gresley BSK, BR Mk 1 CK, Stanier BSK, SK – BR maroon
DATE: 1964 **SERVICE:** Crewe-Aberdeen **LOCATION:** Beattock

BR 'Britannia' 4-6-2 BR lined green, late crests (Hornby), Stanier Period III BSK, SK, SK, SK, CK, CK, SK, SK, BSK – BR maroon
DATE: 1965 **SERVICE:** Glasgow-Euston **LOCATION:** Carlisle

Class 40 BR green with small yellow panels (Bachmann/Hornby), Stanier Period III BSK, BR Mk 1 SK, CK, RB, FO, BSK – BR maroon
DATE: 1965 **SERVICE:** Euston-Carlisle **LOCATION:** Lune Gorge

SUITABLE 'OO' GAUGE PASSENGER COACHING STOCK

TYPE	COLOUR SCHEME	MANUFACTURER	CAT NO.
BR Mk 2 BFK	BR blue/grey	Bachmann	39-410A
BR Mk 2 BSO	BR blue/grey	Bachmann	39-380A
BR Mk 2 FK	BR blue/grey	Bachmann	39-332A
BR Mk 2 TSO	BR blue/grey	Bachmann	39-360C
BR Mk 2 TSO	BR NSE	Bachmann	39-363A
BR Mk 2a TSO	BR blue/grey	Bachmann	39-360B
BR Mk 2d BSO	BR blue/grey	Hornby	R4563
BR Mk 2d BSO	BR InterCity	Dapol	E15
BR Mk 2d BSO	InterCity 'Swallow'	Hornby	R4464A
BR Mk 2d BSO	Virgin Trains	Hornby	R4087E
BR Mk 2d FO	BR blue/grey	Hornby	R4215C
BR Mk 2d FO	BR InterCity	Dapol	E13
BR Mk 2d FO	InterCity 'Swallow'	Hornby	R4462A
BR MK 2d FO	Virgin Trains	Hornby	R4088D
BR Mk 2d TSO	BR blue/grey	Hornby	R4216C
BR Mk 2d TSO	BR InterCity	Dapol	E14
BR Mk 2d TSO	InterCity 'Swallow'	Hornby	R4463C
BR MK 2d TSO	Virgin Trains	Hornby	R4086H
BR Mk 2e BSO	BR blue/grey	Hornby	R4615
BR Mk 2e BSO	InterCity 'Swallow'	Hornby	R4618
BR Mk 2e BSO	Virgin Trains	Hornby	R4704
BR Mk 2e FO	BR blue/grey	Hornby	R4614
BR Mk 2e FO	InterCity 'Swallow'	Hornby	R4617
BR Mk 2e TSO	BR blue/grey	Hornby	R4613
BR Mk 2e TSO	InterCity 'Swallow'	Hornby	R4614
BR Mk 2e TSO	Virgin Trains	Hornby	R4702/A

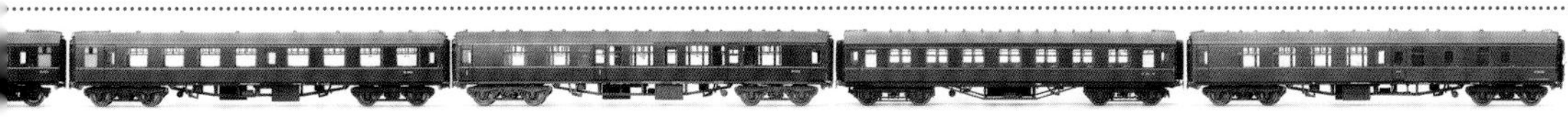

TRAIN FORMATIONS

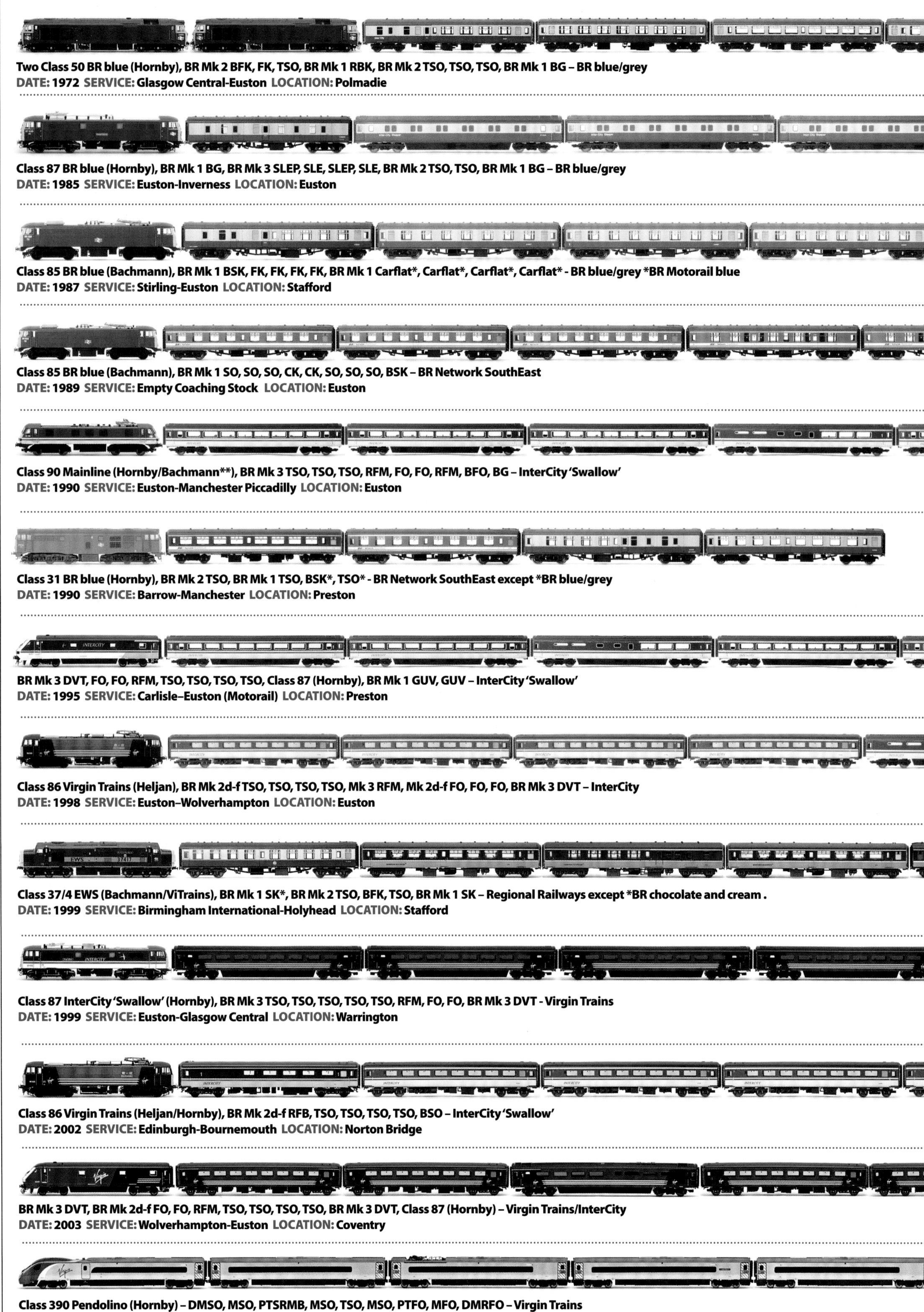

Two Class 50 BR blue (Hornby), BR Mk 2 BFK, FK, TSO, BR Mk 1 RBK, BR Mk 2 TSO, TSO, TSO, BR Mk 1 BG – BR blue/grey
DATE: 1972 **SERVICE:** Glasgow Central-Euston **LOCATION:** Polmadie

Class 87 BR blue (Hornby), BR Mk 1 BG, BR Mk 3 SLEP, SLE, SLEP, SLE, BR Mk 2 TSO, TSO, BR Mk 1 BG – BR blue/grey
DATE: 1985 **SERVICE:** Euston-Inverness **LOCATION:** Euston

Class 85 BR blue (Bachmann), BR Mk 1 BSK, FK, FK, FK, FK, BR Mk 1 Carflat*, Carflat*, Carflat*, Carflat* - BR blue/grey *BR Motorail blue
DATE: 1987 **SERVICE:** Stirling-Euston **LOCATION:** Stafford

Class 85 BR blue (Bachmann), BR Mk 1 SO, SO, SO, CK, CK, SO, SO, SO, BSK – BR Network SouthEast
DATE: 1989 **SERVICE:** Empty Coaching Stock **LOCATION:** Euston

Class 90 Mainline (Hornby/Bachmann), BR Mk 3 TSO, TSO, TSO, RFM, FO, FO, RFM, BFO, BG – InterCity 'Swallow'**
DATE: 1990 **SERVICE:** Euston-Manchester Piccadilly **LOCATION:** Euston

Class 31 BR blue (Hornby), BR Mk 2 TSO, BR Mk 1 TSO, BSK*, TSO* - BR Network SouthEast except *BR blue/grey
DATE: 1990 **SERVICE:** Barrow-Manchester **LOCATION:** Preston

BR Mk 3 DVT, FO, FO, RFM, TSO, TSO, TSO, TSO, Class 87 (Hornby), BR Mk 1 GUV, GUV – InterCity 'Swallow'
DATE: 1995 **SERVICE:** Carlisle–Euston (Motorail) **LOCATION:** Preston

Class 86 Virgin Trains (Heljan), BR Mk 2d-f TSO, TSO, TSO, TSO, Mk 3 RFM, Mk 2d-f FO, FO, FO, BR Mk 3 DVT – InterCity
DATE: 1998 **SERVICE:** Euston–Wolverhampton **LOCATION:** Euston

Class 37/4 EWS (Bachmann/ViTrains), BR Mk 1 SK*, BR Mk 2 TSO, BFK, TSO, BR Mk 1 SK – Regional Railways except *BR chocolate and cream .
DATE: 1999 **SERVICE:** Birmingham International-Holyhead **LOCATION:** Stafford

Class 87 InterCity 'Swallow' (Hornby), BR Mk 3 TSO, TSO, TSO, TSO, TSO, RFM, FO, FO, BR Mk 3 DVT - Virgin Trains
DATE: 1999 **SERVICE:** Euston-Glasgow Central **LOCATION:** Warrington

Class 86 Virgin Trains (Heljan/Hornby), BR Mk 2d-f RFB, TSO, TSO, TSO, TSO, BSO – InterCity 'Swallow'
DATE: 2002 **SERVICE:** Edinburgh-Bournemouth **LOCATION:** Norton Bridge

BR Mk 3 DVT, BR Mk 2d-f FO, FO, RFM, TSO, TSO, TSO, TSO, BR Mk 3 DVT, Class 87 (Hornby) – Virgin Trains/InterCity
DATE: 2003 **SERVICE:** Wolverhampton-Euston **LOCATION:** Coventry

Class 390 Pendolino (Hornby) – DMSO, MSO, PTSRMB, MSO, TSO, MSO, PTFO, MFO, DMRFO – Virgin Trains
DATE: 2007 **SERVICE:** Euston-Manchester Piccadilly **LOCATION:** Nuneaton

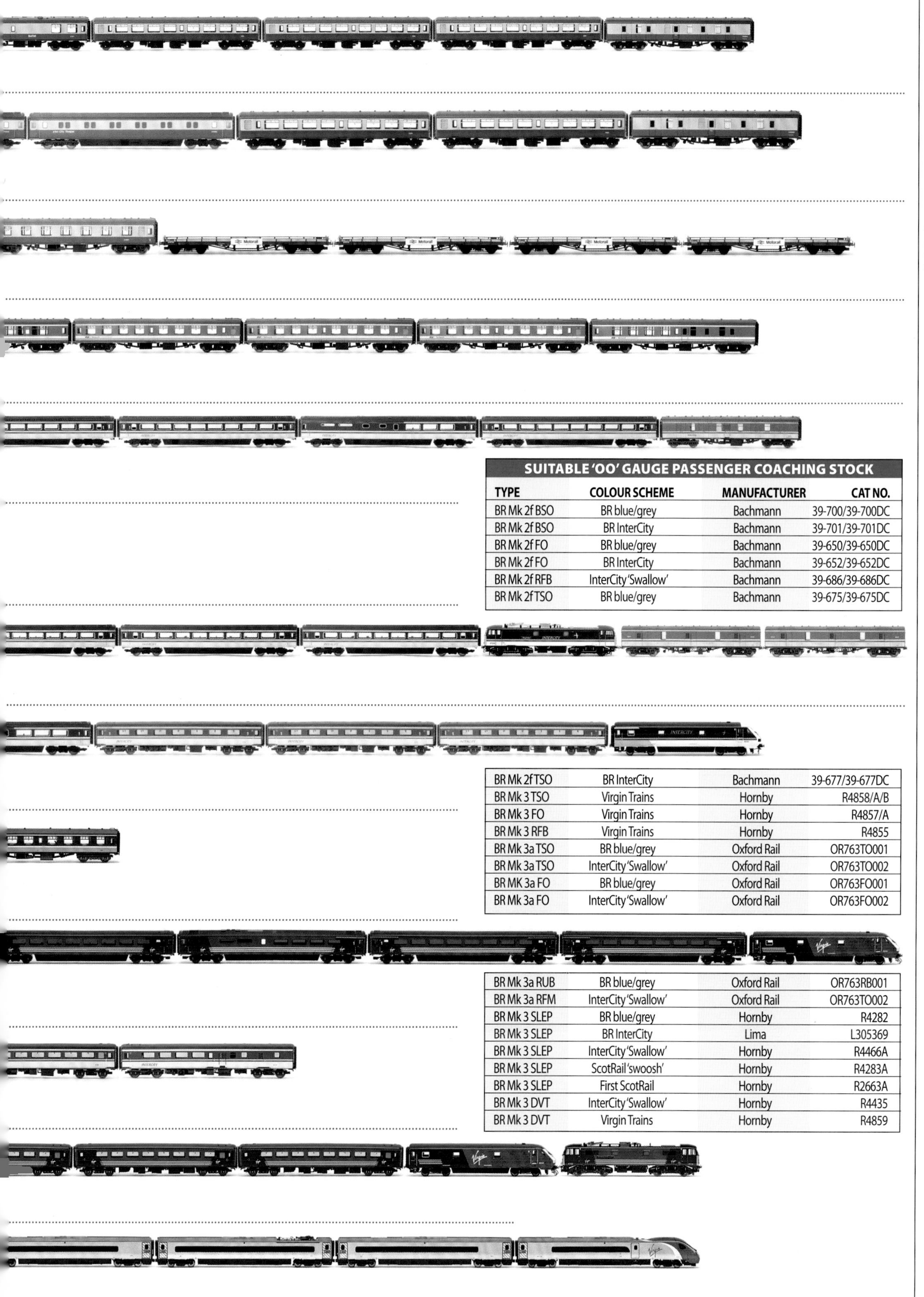

SUITABLE 'OO' GAUGE PASSENGER COACHING STOCK

TYPE	COLOUR SCHEME	MANUFACTURER	CAT NO.
BR Mk 2f BSO	BR blue/grey	Bachmann	39-700/39-700DC
BR Mk 2f BSO	BR InterCity	Bachmann	39-701/39-701DC
BR Mk 2f FO	BR blue/grey	Bachmann	39-650/39-650DC
BR Mk 2f FO	BR InterCity	Bachmann	39-652/39-652DC
BR Mk 2f RFB	InterCity 'Swallow'	Bachmann	39-686/39-686DC
BR Mk 2f TSO	BR blue/grey	Bachmann	39-675/39-675DC
BR Mk 2f TSO	BR InterCity	Bachmann	39-677/39-677DC
BR Mk 3 TSO	Virgin Trains	Hornby	R4858/A/B
BR Mk 3 FO	Virgin Trains	Hornby	R4857/A
BR Mk 3 RFB	Virgin Trains	Hornby	R4855
BR Mk 3a TSO	BR blue/grey	Oxford Rail	OR763TO001
BR Mk 3a TSO	InterCity 'Swallow'	Oxford Rail	OR763TO002
BR MK 3a FO	BR blue/grey	Oxford Rail	OR763FO001
BR Mk 3a FO	InterCity 'Swallow'	Oxford Rail	OR763FO002
BR Mk 3a RUB	BR blue/grey	Oxford Rail	OR763RB001
BR Mk 3a RFM	InterCity 'Swallow'	Oxford Rail	OR763TO002
BR Mk 3 SLEP	BR blue/grey	Hornby	R4282
BR Mk 3 SLEP	BR InterCity	Lima	L305369
BR Mk 3 SLEP	InterCity 'Swallow'	Hornby	R4466A
BR Mk 3 SLEP	ScotRail 'swoosh'	Hornby	R4283A
BR Mk 3 SLEP	First ScotRail	Hornby	R2663A
BR Mk 3 DVT	InterCity 'Swallow'	Hornby	R4435
BR Mk 3 DVT	Virgin Trains	Hornby	R4859

Masterpieces in the GALLERY

We present a selection of the best layouts and model photography from the past year in *Hornby Magazine*.

Carl Woodwards' 'N' gauge exhibition layout, Vale of Oxbury, is a stunning showcase of the powers of 2mm scale. The entire layout measures just 12ft x 4ft, yet it has a feeling of being much larger. Here a Blue Pullman DEMU thunders towards the station as a Collett 'Grange' 4-6-0 departs with a milk working. Meanwhile a Class 121 waits on the branch for a path into the station. Vale of Oxbury featured in HM133. Trevor Jones/*Hornby Magazine*.

At Southwick a Bulleid air-smoothed 'Merchant Navy' 4-6-2 leads an express through the platforms and past the signalbox at this busy Southern Region junction station. Southwick, built in 'OO' gauge, is owned and operated by the Marlow, Maidenhead and District Model Railway Club. It featured in HM131. Trevor Jones/*Hornby Magazine*.

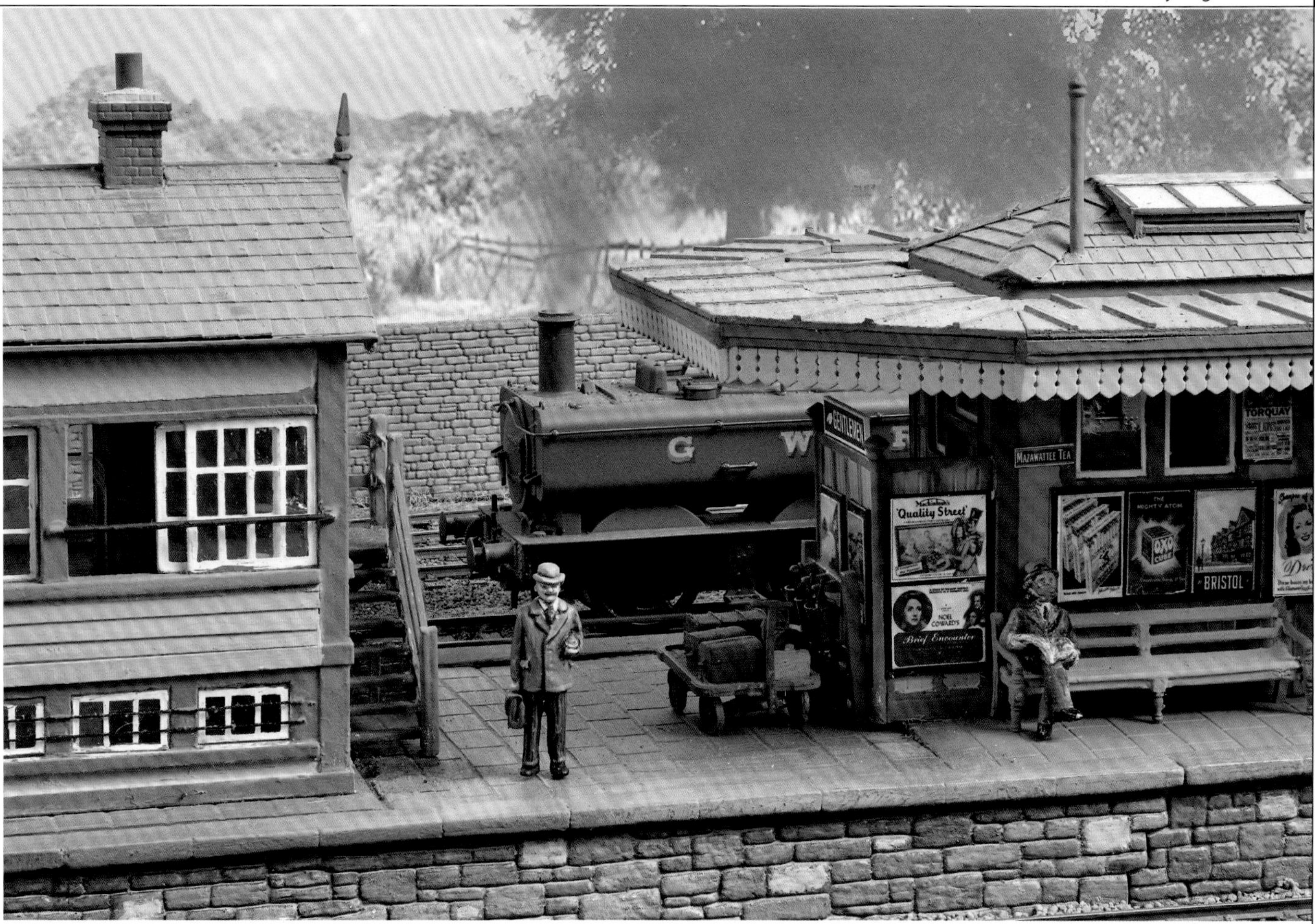

Above: **A Nod to Brent is Robin Sweet's home based 'OO' gauge layout which measures 14ft x 7ft and includes a busy main line station set in the last years of the Great Western Railway. Here a GWR '64XX' 0-6-0PT simmers in the loop behind the station awaiting its next call of duty. A Nod to Brent featured in HM126.** Trevor Jones/*Hornby Magazine.*

Below: **David Dann-Gibbons set out to recreate the Great Central Railway London Extension at Wendover in 'OO' gauge and elected to model it mainly in the LNER period. Great Central Railway 'B2' 4-6-0 427 *City of London* passes through with a sleeping car train. Wendover featured in HM135.** Trevor Jones/*Hornby Magazine.*

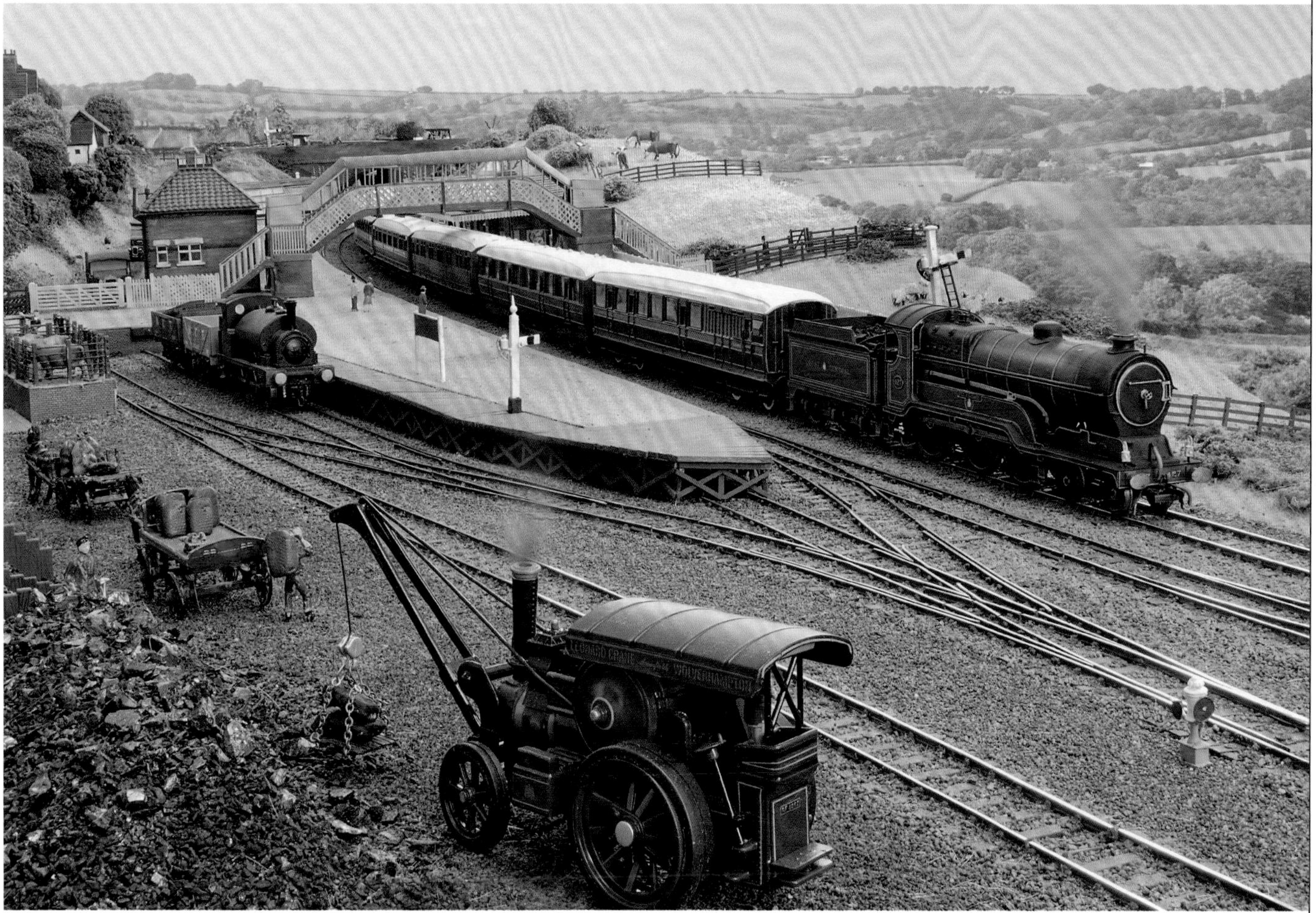

The West Country is the location of Paul Toulmin's evocative 1970s period 'OO' gauge layout Exeter Junction. As well as featuring a busy station and depot scene on one side, it also models open country with a double track main line running through. On a fine summer Saturday Class 45 1-Co-Co-1 37 tackles the gradient with a long rake of BR blue and grey Mk 1s. Exeter Junction featured in HM136. Mike Wild/*Hornby Magazine*.

1E
02
37

The Somerset Railway Modellers Group has recreated part of the Taunton-Barnstaple route in the 1960s in 'OO' gauge when Western and Southern region stock ran side by side. Oake may not have existed in real life, but the line did and all train movements are matched to those which took place on the real line. As a Pressed Steel Class 121 departs, a Maunsell 'N' 2-6-0 heads south for Taunton. Oake featured in HM134. Trevor Jones/*Hornby Magazine.*

Below: **The Summit is Yeovil Model Railway Club's impressive 'O' gauge exhibition layout which measures 47ft x 27ft. It models the Settle and Carlisle line, but due to the open nature of the scenery its period of operation varies. In LMS days a Stanier 'Jubilee' 4-6-0 works north as a Bowen-Cooke 'Super D' 0-8-0 plods south over one of the culverts. The Summit featured in HM127.** Trevor Jones/*Hornby Magazine.*

Whiteacres is Stafford Model Railway Circle's latest 'OO' gauge modern image layout which sets out to capture the colourful and busy nature of the railways in the early 2000s. Cement wagons are propelled to the loading point in the foreground by a Class 08 while a Class 66 is about to pass under the main line with a Class 60 heading a coal working above. Whiteacres featured in HM129. Trevor Jones/*Hornby Magazine*.

John Emerson bid farewell to his long standing 'O' gauge, and once exhibition layout, Gifford Street in 2018 to make way for his latest Western Region project in the same scale. Class 40 D211 *Mauretania* – a Heljan model with added detail and weathering – thunders past the British Diecast Corporation factory with a Travelling Post Office working. Gifford Street featured in HM135. Mike Wild/*Hornby Magazine*.

Starting out in NARROW GAUGE

The arrival of Bachmann's first ready-to-run 'OO9' steam locomotive is an exciting catalyst for narrow gauge modelling. **MIKE WILD** explores the subject and discusses how to get started with your own project.

Right: **Roco's 2017 starter set included a Henschel 0-6-0T, four timber wagons, a circuit of set track and an analogue controller. It provides an ideal entry point for a first time narrow gauge layout builder.**

Below: **Bob Vaughan's 'OO9' exhibition layout Tansey Bank (HM76) is a brilliant example of the detail and character possible with narrow gauge layouts. This layout consists of a terminus station, goods facilities and an engine shed too.**

NARROW GAUGE modelling hasn't always been the easiest subject to get into. While there has been longstanding support for the scale in the kit market – and through the OO9 Society – ready-to-run products have been few and far between, especially British prototypes, making it less appealing as a first time model railway project.

Aging 'N' gauge chassis have often been the basis for kit locomotives and in the present day world where we expect locomotives to be Digital Command Control compatible, outdated mechanisms aren't a great draw. In Europe and further afield there is strong support from ready-to-run products including high detail models by Roco and an extensive range from Minitrains to name just two.

On the up side, British outline 'OO9' looks set for a new lease of life with the arrival of Bachmann's first ready-to-run steam locomotive for the gauge - the Baldwin 10-12-D 4-6-0T. It models a 2ft gauge locomotive suitable for a wide range of prototypes including trench railways, quarries, preservation scenes and more besides. Better still, it features working lights, a coreless motor, a Next18 decoder socket and a factory installed speaker in the bunker matching the specification of the latest Bachmann/Graham Farish 'N' gauge locomotives.

The Baldwin tank isn't the only new steam locomotive of British outline for 'OO9' to be released in 2018 though, as Heljan has delivered a small first batch of its Manning Wardle Lynton and Barnstaple Railway 2-6-2Ts, though they sold just as quickly as they arrived in the shops. Happily more are in production for release in late 2018.

Origins

'OO9' uses 9mm gauge track while the scale is identical to 'OO' gauge – 4mm:1ft. By using 9mm gauge track it is used to represent British outline narrow gauge railways built to 2ft and 2ft 6in gauge.

This combination allows a large range of prototypes to be modelled including the famous Ffestiniog Railway, the Welsh Highland Railway, the Vale of Rheidol, Corris Railway, Talyllyn Railway and many more. The same gauge was also used for a large number of narrow gauge industrial railways as well as lightly laid contractor's lines making the possibilities near endless. Plus, with railways like the Lynton and Barnstaple Railway which had a main line connection at Barnstaple, narrow gauge lines can be used as feeder lines to standard gauge railways too.

The world is yours when it comes to narrow gauge railways and, by their nature, they often employed a variety of locomotive designs from different sources. Some were even brought in from overseas, such as the Baldwin 4-6-0Ts by Bachmann, while other home-grown designs became firm favourites on industrial lines. One such locomotive is the Quarry Hunslet 0-4-0ST which is also being developed as a ready-to-run model of 'OO9' by Bachmann.

So where do you start when it comes to 'OO9'? There are three routes to a working railway using 9mm gauge track: a train set to create a new layout, devising a scene using the Peco range of flexible track and points for narrow gauge or alternatively by adding a narrow gauge line into a larger 'OO' gauge main line layout as a feeder route.

Train sets are few and far between, and currently non-existent with British outline rolling stock. Roco has offered a number of starter sets for 'OO9' over the years and its current set (Cat No. 31030) contains a Henschel 0-6-0T, four timber wagons, a circuit of Roco 'OO9' set track and an analogue controller. This is a great way to start any new project and handily the track is compatible with the Peco range too allowing it to be expanded simply.

'OO9' track has different sleeper spacing to 'N' gauge 9mm gauge track, even though they are the same gauge, to reflect the style of the real railways. Roco and Peco both produce comprehensive ranges including points, curves, straights and flexible track meaning that the only limit is your imagination – and space, of course.

Adding a narrow gauge feeder railway to an existing 'OO' gauge layout is another great way to begin indulging in 'OO9'. You won't need a » great deal of stock to start with either keeping costs down while allowing experimentation with its potential. You could build a line as part of a quarry to deliver stone from the face to the crushing plant for further transport by rail or you could develop a multi-modal interchange where standard gauge and narrow gauge meet at a wharf with river or canal boats thrown into the mix too.

Building a railway

The foundations of any model railway, no matter what the scale, need to be firm and stable. Wooden baseboards will be ideal for 'OO9', though alternatives such as foam board could be used too if built with a suitable structure underneath.

Laying the track involves the same processes too requiring underlay such as cork sheet cut to shape, track pins and a pin hammer to tack the track into place on the baseboard. The difference is that narrow gauge railways can negotiate tighter curves than standard gauge lines allowing a winding route to be modelled more accurately in a shorter length. It is even possible to fit a complete circle in just under 2ft, as shown to great effect by Bob Vaughan's test track Hobbs Row Halt (HM74).

Continuous run and terminus layouts are both equally viable in narrow gauge, though you will need to maintain the track and locomotives to a high standard for reliable operation in the case of the latter. For a first 'OO9' project, a continuous run with shunting opportunities will provide the best value. 'Rabbit warren' layouts can be considered too where the railway changes height and crosses over itself opening up a world of fascinating track plan potential.

Beyond the basics of track and ballast, 'OO' 4mm scale buildings, structures, figures, road vehicles and accessories can be used to detail the land around the railway, though there are also ready made buildings by Bachmann built specifically to suit narrow gauge railways and Noch produces a selection of narrow gauge structures too which are available through Gaugemaster.

Developing a fleet

Alongside the Bachmann Baldwin 4-6-0T there is a growing range of narrow gauge ready-to-run locomotives available from Minitrains as well as the previously mentioned Roco product range which focuses on locomotive designs from mainland Europe. Some will look out of place on a British outline layout, but others can be anglicised to fit in on an industrial layout. Beyond this there is also the Quarry Hunslet to look forward to from Bachmann in the future, but if you are looking for a specific locomotive class, kit or scratch building is going to be the way forward.

Happily when it comes to rolling stock there is much more choice. Bachmann has produced open and closed bogie wagons to go with its 4-6-0T and it is also producing slate wagons and an Ashover Light Railway bogie carriage. Peco has been gradually increasing an attractive range of 'OO9' carriages and wagons with models based

USEFUL LINKS	
Bachmann	www.bachmann.co.uk
Backwoods Miniatures	www.bachwoodsminiatures.com
Dundas Models	www.dundasmodels.co.uk
Fourdees	www.fourdees.co.uk
Gaugemaster	www.gaugemaster.com
Heljan	www.heljan.dk
Narrow Planet	www.narrowplanet.co.uk
Nine-Lines	www.nine-lines.co.uk
OO9 Society	www.009society.com
Peco	www.peco-uk.com
Robex Models	www.robexmodels.ch
RT Models	www.rtmodels.co.uk

Right: **A continuous run layout will be simpler to operate and maintain for a first 'OO9' project. To test models for his main layout, Tansey Bank, Bob Vaughan built this circular layout to allow new motive power to be run in.**

Below: **Bachmann has developed a series of resin Scenecraft buildings suitable for use with narrow gauge prototypes. The first set was based on Lynton and Barnstaple Railway structures including Woody Bay station building. Here the Bachmann Baldwin 4-6-0T poses with a goods working while the Roco Henschel stands outside the Scenecraft locomotive shed.**

on the Lynton and Barnstaple and Glynn Valley Tramway vehicles amongst others. Peco also produces slate wagons – a must for any Welsh narrow gauge layout – together with four-wheel hoppers, bolster wagons and Lynton and Barnstaple open and closed wagons. The wagons produced by Roco and Minitrains are also well worth considering as with careful selection there are vehicles which will suit British outline layouts.

There is also a large range of kits available for wagons and coaches - the most accessible being those by Dundas Models. If you have more skills in kit building, the Backwoods Miniatures website is well worth visiting.

Take your pick

There is huge potential for layout design and operation in narrow gauge and with the influx of new British ready-to-run products from Bachmann and Peco the incentive to build a narrow gauge layout is growing stronger. We've seen many brilliant 'OO9' layouts at exhibitions and we only expect to see more in the coming months as more modellers take advantage of this increasing range of high fidelity products. ■

Chris Bone's St Jude's home layout has been updated with the addition of a narrow gauge feeder line alongside the standard gauge route. St Jude's featured in HM139.

West Coast Cement THE FLEET

Turning the clock forward from our usual 1950s subjects has meant developing a new roster of locomotives and rolling stock for our project layout, West Coast Cement. **MIKE WILD** reveals how this new 'OO' gauge fleet has been created to represent the 1995-2005 period.

PRESENTING any new layout brings its own challenges when it comes to locomotives and rolling stock but when we selected the 1995-2005 period for West Coast Cement we had to think long and hard about how we would stock it even before we started laying track. Fortunately both Mark Chivers and I are great collectors and over the years we have amassed large rosters which cover areas well outside the main time period that we have portrayed on *Hornby Magazine's* exhibition layouts so far.

The 10 year period we had chosen offered great scope for variety. We could represent outgoing BR sectorisation period liveries including InterCity, Regional Railways and Railfreight triple grey as well as covering the first shadow privatisation colour schemes of Mainline blue, Transrail branded triple grey and, a personal favourite, Loadhaul black and orange. Added to this we were looking forward to showcasing the early years of privatisation including introducing the new corporate colours of national freight operator English, Welsh & Scottish Railway (EWS) together with West Coast Main Line passenger operator Virgin Trains as well as the likes of Direct Rail Services, Freightliner and Railtrack/Network Rail.

One of the great advantages of the period and location chosen were our own recollections of the line in that period. Holiday breaks took in the likes of Penrith, Oxenholme and Carlisle while day trips included visits to Wigan, Crewe and Preston amongst others where it was possible to observe the West Coast Main Line (WCML) first-hand.

Amongst the catalysts for this layout were the in-development models of the Class 87 by

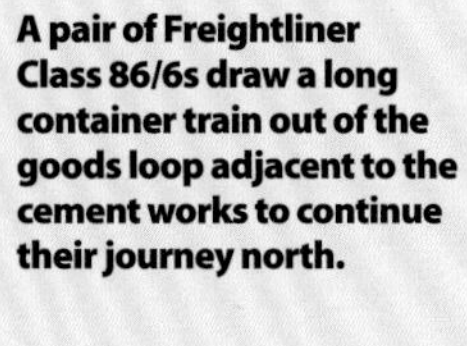

A pair of Freightliner Class 86/6s draw a long container train out of the goods loop adjacent to the cement works to continue their journey north.

Class 37/ 37043 powers along the main line with a rake of Bachmann TTA four-wheel fuel tankers.

Hornby and Class 90 by Bachmann. Both of these overhead AC electric locomotives are essential components of any successful WCML layout and the Class 87 arrived at just the right moment to take part in our final photo shoots. The Class 90 is a few months away, but Bachmann is expecting its highly specified model to arrive in March 2019.

Also essential for the WCML was the Class 86 and we are able to field three for the layout – two in Freightliner green which will run as a pair and one in Virgin Trains black and red. All three are Heljan models and they will be joined by Hornby Class 90s for the initial shows, hopefully with a few added details, and two new Hornby Class 87s to represent the overhead fleet.

Diesel traction

While the WCML has been fully electrified to Glasgow since 1974 it has always seen diesel locomotives operating under the wires alongside electric locomotives. The 1995-2005 period gives a wide range of options for revenue earning trains including classes 20/3, 31, 37, 47, 56, 57, 60, 66, and 67. We haven't got any Direct Rail Services (DRS) Class 20/3s at present, but we can field all the rest plus we have the option to include a West Coast Railways Class 33, 37 or 47 on charter trains.

Class 31s were a rare breed in the late 1990s, but the handful that were still in operation were usually seen around the North West. A trip to Ellesmere Port netted one of the last BR blue liveried examples in around 1998 while an adventure to Wigan the same year saw another »

four examples in service including a pair in 'Dutch' grey and yellow together with 31201 in Railfreight Coal sector livery and 31420 in mainline colours.

The fleet for West Coast Cement will include a 'Dutch' and a Regional Railways liveried example initially, as the class would have been a rarity in the area we intend West Coast Cement to be located. Both are equipped with Hornby Twin Track Sound decoders with the speakers upgraded to Zimo 40mm x 20mm single-driver 3D printed examples.

The go-anywhere Class 37 was still an everyday sight on the main line network in the late 1990s and they could be seen on all types of duty from heavy freights to passenger work on the North Wales coast and 'sleeper' trains in Scotland. During the period we are modelling the range of liveries carried by the Class 37 fleet was impressive to say the least and included 'Dutch' grey and yellow, Railfreight triple grey with sector markings, the same colour schemes with Trainsrail logos, Loadhaul black and orange, Mainline blue, EWS maroon and gold, Regional Railways, InterCity and heritage liveries including BR 'large logo' blue (37408) and BR green (37411).

Choosing which of these to represent was a difficult task, but to get the ball rolling we will be running 37422 *Robert F Fairlie* in Regional Railways livery fitted with a Howes Models LokSound decoder, 37254 in 'Dutch' grey and yellow with a Bachmann LokSound decoder, 37242 in Mainline blue with a Bachmann LokSound decoder, 37521 *English China Clays* in EWS maroon and gold with a LokSound decoder – all Bachmann locomotives – plus 37417 in EWS maroon and gold fitted with a Hornby Twin Track Sound decoder and upgraded speaker. »

WEST COAST CEMENT LOCOMOTIVE ROSTER

CLASS	IDENTITY	LIVERY	DECODER
Class 31/4	31439 *North Yorkshire Moors Railway*	Regional Railways	Hornby TTS
Class 31/0	31110	'Dutch' grey and yellow	Hornby TTS
Class 37/0	37043	'Dutch' grey and yellow	Bachmann LokSound
Class 37/0	37242	Mainline blue	Bachmann LokSound
Class 37/0	37254	'Dutch' grey and yellow	Legomanbiffo LokSound
Class 37/4	37417 *Richard Trevithick*	EWS maroon and gold	Hornby TTS
Class 37/4	37422 *Robert F Fairlie*	Regional Railways	Howes LokSound
Class 37/5	37521 *English China Clays*	EWS maroon and gold	Bachmann LokSound
Class 43	43103 *John Wesley*/43194	InterCity	ZImo MX645R x2
Class 47/0	47209 *Herbert Austin*	Railfreight Distribution	Hatton's 21-pin
Class 47/0	47365 *Diamond Jubilee*	Railfreight Distribution	Hatton's 21-pin
Class 47/7	47745 *Royal Society for the Blind*	RES red and grey	Bachmann 21-pin
Class 47/8	47844 *Derby and Derbyshire Chamber of Commerce and Industry*	InterCity	Hornby TTS
Class 56	56003	Loadhaul black and orange	Zimo MX645R
Class 56	56095 *Harworth Colliery*	Railfreight coal sector	Legomanbiffo LokSound
Class 56	56103 *Stora*	EWS maroon and gold	Legomanbiffo LokSound
Class 57/0	57003 *Freightliner Evolution*	Freightliner green and yellow	Bachmann LokSound
Class 60	60007	Loadhaul black and orange	Hornby TTS
Class 60	60014 *Alexander Fleming*	Railfreight metals sector	Hornby TTS
Class 60	60033 *Tees Steel Express*	One-off blue	Hornby TTS
Class 60	60048 *Eastern*	EWS maroon and gold	Hornby LokSound
Class 66	66111	EWS maroon and gold	Bachmann LokSound
Class 66	66200	EWS maroon and gold	Bachmann LokSound
Class 66	66522	Freightliner Shanks green	Legmanbiffo LokSound
Class 67	67016	EWS maroon and gold	Hornby TTS
Class 86	86205 *City of Lancaster*	Virgin Trains	Hatton's 8-pin harness
Class 86/6	86605	Freightliner green and yellow	Hatton's 8-pin harness
Class 86/6	86635	Freightliner green and yellow	Hatton's 8-pin harness
Class 87	87010 *King Arthur*	InterCity	DCC Concepts Zen Nano
Class 87	87031 *Hal 'O The Wynd*	InterCity	DCC Concepts Zen Nano
Class 90	90128	Belgian Railways blue and yellow	Hatton's 8-pin harness
Class 90	90131	Railfreight Distribution	Hatton's 8-pin harness
Class 92	92016 *Brahms*	EWS branded triple grey	Hornby R8249
Class 150/2	150270	Regional Railways	Bachmann 21-pin
Class 153	153303	Regional Railways	Hatton's 8-pin harness
Class 221	221130	Virgin Trains	TBA
Class 390	390012 *Virgin Star*	Virgin Trains	Hatton's 8-pin harness x2

Class 56 56095 *Harworth Colliery* ticks over in the goods loop waiting for an express to pass while Class 37242 stands in the cement works yard. The signals are Train-Tech sensor signals which automatically switch from green to red when a train passes and then cycle through the sequence back to green.

Class 43 HST power car 43103 *John Wesley* leads a Virgin CrossCountry 2+7 formation past the cement works while Class 56 56003 waits with loaded tanks in the exchange sidings. The powers cars and Class 56 are all fitted with Zimo MX645R decoders.

87010 *King Arthur* heads south as Class 60 60048 *Eastern* passes in the opposite direction. In the cement works a Class 08 is busy shunting while a Class 66 waits to take the next loaded departure.

Like the Class 37, Class 47s were regularly used across the railway network in the late 1990s. They weren't as common on the northern section of the West Coast Main Line, but nevertheless we thought they were important enough on the railway scene to be represented on West Coast Cement. Our fleet includes examples in Rail Express Systems red and grey, Railfreight triple grey with Distribution markings, Railfreight Distribution grey, InterCity and Virgin Trains colours. The latter will be used on locomotive hauled CrossCountry workings – a slight extension of reality – to add variety to passenger services taking turns at the head of a rake of Mk 2e stock in InterCity and Virgin Trains colours.

Heavy freight power

Class 56s were regular performers on the route and again we have a healthy selection available for the future. The first to be prepared include 56003 in Loadhaul black and orange equipped with a Zimo MX645R decoder and 40mm x 22mm twin-driver speaker, 56095 *Harworth Colliery* in Railfreight Coal sector triple grey fitted with a Legomanbiffo ESU LokSound decoder and EM1 speaker plus 56103 *Stora* in EWS maroon and gold which is being fitted with the same decoder and speaker combination as 56095.

The Class 57 Co-Co diesels – re-engineered Class 47s with EMD engines built by Brush in Loughborough – were introduced in 1998 and, as such, we will have a couple of early examples on the roster in Freightliner green and yellow. Again they would have been comparatively rare on the northern section of the WCML as most container trains were handled by electric traction on this part of the route.

The line had its fair share of heavy freight traffic including bulk flows such as coal and cement. Class 56s were regulars on these flows, but the powerful 3,300hp Class 60s were also used for coal and cement traffic on the route. West Coast Cement's Class 60 fleet will include versions in Railfreight triple grey with sector markings, Loadhaul black and orange, Mainline blue, EWS maroon and gold and one-off blue liveried 60033 *Tees Steel Express*. All those operating on the layout will be equipped with Hornby Twin Track Sound decoders connected to uprated Zimo 40mm x 20mm single-driver 3D printed speakers.

Modelling this period means that as well as representing the soon to be withdrawn Class 31s and 37s we can also utilise the new breed of General Motors Class 66 and 67 diesel-electrics. The first of the Class 66s arrived with EWS for testing in 1998 and, almost 20 years later, these Co-Co locomotives are now the dominant face of freight traffic in the UK. EWS was soon followed by Freightliner which ordered its first five Class 66/5s in 1998 and we will be representing both fleets on West Coast Cement using Bachmann models in both colour schemes including 66522 in Freightliner Shanks colours.

Joining them will be the 1999-2000 introduced Class 67 high-speed diesel-electrics which were built by Alsthom in Spain using General Motors engines. They were designed to replace Class 47/7s on mail traffic initially – though later they were found on intermodal, charter and other duties. EWS and Royal Train liveried examples will operate on West Coast Cement, all equipped with Hornby Twin Track Sound decoders and Zimo speakers.

EWS Class 66 66200 rounds the curve under the dual carriageway with a rake of Bachmann IPA car carrying wagons.

Class 37s 37521 *English China Clays* and 37254 power up to draw a fresh cut of wagons out of the cement works sidings.

In the cement works Class 56 56003 carefully rolls into the sidings with a rake of empty PCA tankers.

The formations

There is plenty of traffic variety to represent on the WCML and the fleet for the layout will include everything from Diesel Multiple Units (DMUs) through to London-Glasgow express passenger workings, heavy freights, Freightliner container trains and ballast traffic.

Passenger formations will be modelled with a selection of Mk 2E and Mk 2F carriages by Hornby and Bachmann respectively together with Hornby Mk 3s for both HST and locomotive hauled workings. These will be presented in InterCity and Virgin Trains colours with some mixed formations typical of the late 1990s.

Joining the long distance trains will be a short Regional Railway set of Mk 1 and Mk 2 non-air conditioned stock – not strictly prototypical, but adding variety – together with Class 150/2 DMUs, a Virgin Voyager four-car unit and, potentially, a nine-car Hornby Virgin Pendolino.

A charter train is also likely to feature in the roster for West Coast Cement allowing the opportunity to run locomotives including Stanier 'Duchess' 46233 *Duchess of Sutherland*, BR '8P' 71000 *Duke of Gloucester*, Gresley 'A4' »

60009 *Union of South Africa* and others.

Freight traffic promises to be diverse. Cement will be a signature of the layout with empty and loaded workings coming and going from the exchange sidings alongside the main line. These will be formed of Bachmann PCAs as well as Hornby depressed centre PCA bulk powder wagons initially. Secondary traffic for the cement works will include VGA vans arriving for loading with bagged cement and incoming supplies of coal which we plan to deliver in a rake of MEA four-wheel box wagons.

Adding variety on the main lines will be intermodal workings, Freightliner trains plus fuel, steel, coal and car trains. We also intend modelling the famed Enterprise workings – short lived modern day wagon load traffic – which can include everything from OTA timber wagons and VGA sliding door vans to Silver Bullet china clay tankers and Cargowaggon flats. Infrastructure trains will be modelled with a block formation of 'Seacow' ballast hoppers, MRA side tipping five-wagon sets and Railtrack Autoballaster rakes.

Starting point

The stock detailed here is just the starting point for West Coast Cement's stock roster as we have more to add as time allows. By the time of the layout's first showing we expect to have more locomotives weathered, possibly the introduction of the Network Rail New Measurement Train, which entered traffic in 2003 using Class 43 HST power cars, a nuclear flask train and more. We will also be looking to expand the cement wagon fleet in 2019 when Accurascale's new PCA wagons become available too

Preparing locomotives, particularly with sound, takes time but we are confident that the variety we have already put together is representative of the time period. It's been an exciting adventure putting together West Coast Cement as a layout just as much as it has been developing the rolling stock and we are looking forward to enhancing, detailing and weathering the entire fleet over time to make it even more comprehensive and accurate for the period. ■

Class 86 86205 *City of Lancaster* (a Heljan model) thunders along the main line with a northbound express destined for Glasgow.

Hornby Class 67 67016, fitted with a Hornby TTS decoder and Zimo 40mm x 20mm speaker, heads a parcels working along the main line.

15 SIMPLE WAYS OF Modelling HOPPER TRAINS

In recent years the introduction of new products from ready-to-run manufacturers has considerably broadened the scope of freight operations, especially in terms of hopper wagons. **TIM SHACKLETON** takes a look at what's possible off the shelf – and what, for the time being, still calls for kit-building skills.

A LOT'S CHANGED in the six decades I've been a railway enthusiast and model-maker. Passenger trains have altered out of all recognition, and so has freight. The once-familiar mixed goods has all but vanished along with wagonload traffic of any description – who sends 60 tons of anything by rail these days? Many bulk commodities – coal, biomass, aggregates, cement, powdered chemicals – are handled in long rakes of bottom-discharge hopper wagons.

When I was young, though, there were far fewer traffic flows using hoppers and it was all very different. I recall endless rows of 21ton hoppers awaiting unloading from the coal staithes at Blyth, ochre-coloured iron ore wagons at Tyne Dock, sheeted 25ton anhydrite hoppers on the Settle and Carlisle line, bulk grain wagons (just like my Hornby Dublo model) at the Co-op flour mills in Sowerby Bridge and lumbering ICI limestone hoppers at Northwich. Everything else, on the whole, seemed to be carried flat on the deck.

Top-loading, bottom-emptying hopper wagons made a lot of operational sense, as American and European railways had long realised. You dropped the load in from the top, usually by mechanical means, and you didn't have to pay men to shovel it out – you simply opened a trap door and out it came in a big rush.

In the North East, shipment coal had always been handled in hopper wagons even before the days of the Stockton & Darlington but other railways were slow to catch on and the 16ton mineral wagon reigned supreme for many years. Even in the late 1950s, hopper wagons for bulk commodities such as cement and iron ore were still something of a novelty and were by and large limited to major customers with the necessary loading and discharge facilities.

Things are very different now. For the thick end of 40 years much of our energy needs have been met using hopper wagons of various kinds and the same is true of other traffics. On the heaviest freight flows only automotive, timber, intermodal, household waste and petrochemicals use anything else. So for this profile I thought we'd look at the range of traffic carried in hopper wagons over the last 60 years or so and the sheer variety of wagon types that's been involved. I can't cover everything, but I hope the examples I give – both prototype and model – will help you decide what's appropriate to your own interests. If I can encourage you to think about ways of upgrading your wagon stock through extra detailing, customisation and especially weathering, then so much the better! ■

Right: **The ICI bogie hoppers were famed for their use on limestone traffic from the Peak District quarries to the ICI plant at Northwich. Introduced in 1936, the last weren't withdrawn until the early 2000s having seen everything from LMS black '8F' 2-8-0s through BR green and blue diesels to sector liveried Class 37s at the head of these heavy trains. In 2018 Hatton's delivered its ready-to-run model of these popular prototypes for 'OO' gauge following a collaboration with Oxford Rail. Here a Hornby Stanier '8F' 2-8-0 leads a rake through Topley Dale on *Hornby Magazine's* test track.**

1. BLAST FROM THE PAST

In my view the best-looking freight trains ever to operate in this country were National Power's solid rakes of JHA/JMA hoppers, used both on coal and limestone traffic. This was as handsome (and consistent) a livery as was carried by many express passenger trains, and a few wagons still retain it, albeit battered and faded. No ready-to-run version of this type has ever been produced. Darryl Smith is building a rake of National Power JMAs using modified Bachmann Freightliner HHAs as the basis – the bodyshells are virtually identical. The tricky part is the bogies, for which he used 3D printed LTF25 bogies from Olympia Models online shop via Shapeways, with 10.5mm disc inside bearing wheels by Colin Craig. Darryl made new corrugated ends from 40 thou Evergreen styrene Metal Siding (2mm spacing). Both inner (with Kadee couplings) and outer wagons with buffers are shown.

2. TYNE DOCK-CONSETT

Among the best-known freight workings of the steam era were the Tyne Dock-Consett iron ore runs using BR-built 56ton wagons that were unique to these operations. Because of the savage prevailing gradients on the line (and the equally fierce winds whipping across the Durham hills), train lengths were severely restricted.

Not surprisingly, no off-the-shelf version of these famous wagons has yet been offered but if Hatton's can produce an ICI hopper and Kernow a 'Clay Tiger', then who knows what the future may hold?

Two excellent 4mm scale kits are available – one (largely in etched brass) from Dave Bradwell and the other, in white metal, from Dave Alexander which is the version shown here. There are quite a few of both on this layout, an 'EM' gauge model of South Pelaw yard built by a group of modellers deep in northern England – it made its first public appearances in 2018. Here an 'O1' 2-8-0 takes a loaded train towards Consett banked by a 'Q7' 0-8-0.

Even modelling the modern privatised railway can quickly become an exercise in nostalgia. It seems incredible that this scene – photographed on June 2 2010 – should already be ancient history. GBRf's Metronet-liveried 66718 *Gwyneth Dunwoody* brings a loaded set of HYA coal hoppers out of the loop at Milford Junction while long rakes of EWS's HTA wagons pack the adjacent sidings, waiting to be reloaded. Due to changes in energy policy, coal traffic has almost vanished from our railways along with many of the wagons themselves while 66718 has become *Sir Peter Hendy OBE*, the black-liveried 'London Sights' locomotive.

3. BALLAST, BACK IN THE DAY

This is how a typical ballast train might have looked at any time between the mid-1950s and the late 1980s. In summer 1982 a Class 40 trundles a splendid array of empty hoppers through Horbury towards Healey Mills yard – a 'Mackerel' (to use these wagons' unique names) a 'Trout', another 'Mackerel', six 'Dogfish', a couple more 'Mackerel', a pair of 'Sealions' and finally four more 'Dogfish'. It's interesting that eight of the ten 'Dogfish' have the distinctive bodyside extensions originally intended to enable them to be used on slag ballast traffic, which had a lower mass for the same volume. This was very much an Eastern/North Eastern development, applied also to the LNER-derived 'Trout'.

Thus inspired, I modified these Hornby 'Trout' ballast hoppers with extended side raves before painting them black and giving them a solid coat of weathering. The interiors and discharge chutes are heavily rusted, as you'd expect from wagons that stood around in all weathers waiting to be loaded.

4. BALLAST TRAINS IN THE 21ST CENTURY

For my money Bachmann's JJA Autoballasters are quite possibly the best and most sophisticated model wagons yet released, rivalled only by Hornby's equally exquisite KFA container flats. Owned originally by Railtrack (whose livery they carry) they're now operated by Network Rail while others were hired in from the now-defunct Carillion. Autoballasters deliver ballast to engineering possessions and operate in rakes of five – one wagon in each set will have a generator to power the lights and other operating features of these massive wagons. Single sets of five are quite common on minor routes but for main line operations you can see them in rakes of 15, 20, 25 and more, sometimes with an odd extra wagon tucked into the formation and sometimes running with non-hopper engineers' wagons as well.

The HQAs were originally introduced to work on Channel Tunnel Rail Link operations (many of them still carry their CTRL set numbers) but can now be seen in all parts of the country.

A point to note is that every Autoballaster in the set will weather in much the same way. The rakes aren't fixed but they'll all have been delivered at much the same time, they'll all have done a similar amount of work and they'll all have been exposed to the same climate.

5. ON FOUR WHEELS

Even in the privatisation era, a surprising number of bulk operations used four-wheel hopper wagons. On July 19 2000, 60023 inches cautiously out of Marks Tey yard near Colchester with a sand train for Hayes. Until the arrival of the EMD Class 66 in the late 1990s, the Brush-built Class 60, along with the earlier Class 56, had a monopoly of heavy-haul operations in the UK.

Hornby's long-established PGA wagon maybe lacks the sophistication of some of their more recent productions but it's still a useful model that – like many products of this period – holds a lot of potential. Cavalex Models is also producing a new ready-to-run model for 'OO' in Redland and LaFarge liveries, but if you have the older Hornby version you will find a wide selection of parts available from small suppliers such as S Kits, Cambrian and Wizard Models/51L that will enable you to upgrade these basic models and introduce interesting prototype variations.

6. MERRY-GO-ROUND

Introduced in the mid-1960s – some even made their delivery runs behind steam locomotives – the 32ton coal hopper was a symbol of Britain's rail freight operation for the best part of four decades. They replaced the 16ton mineral wagon on power station coal traffic until they in turn were superseded around the turn of the century by a new generation of 102ton hoppers, now themselves largely redundant.

I love the feeling of purposefulness as de-branded triple grey livery 56062 *Mountsorrel* powers through Burton Salmon on June 2 1994 – almost a quarter-century ago! – with another load of furnace coal for one of the Aire Valley power stations in Yorkshire.

Running in rakes of 30-40 wagons, the HAAs (as they were coded under TOPS) have long been a favourite among modellers in 'OO' and 'N' gauges. For much of their careers there was always an intriguing variety of liveries on view even though the wagons themselves were to all intents and purposes identical. These are the original Hornby models with scale wheels and much additional detailing.

The Tyne Dock-Consett iron ore trains were restricted in length because of the severe gradients on the line and used specially designed 56ton hopper wagons. Here, with Stella Flats in the distance, a '9F' 2-10-0 blasts out of South Pelaw where it will have paused to take on a banker in the late 1960s.

7. CHEMISTRY LESSON

In steam days coal was the main traffic carried in block trains but other flows used hopper wagons as well. 'Covhops', as a case in point, were often used to transport powdered chemicals in bulk. Throughout their 30-year career on BR these wagons could often be seen running singly or in twos and threes but most of them tended to be allocated to circuit workings to and from such destinations as Trafford Park, Northwich, Corkickle and Port Sunlight, and were branded accordingly.

Bachmann's 4mm scale 'Covhop' is an excellent model that benefits from heavy weathering – the corrosive nature of their loads ensured the paint finish was anything but pristine.

The need for a roof is obvious but other, less volatile chemicals could be transported in open hopper wagons that were sheeted at all times to prevent water ingress. The best-known were probably the vacuum-braked 25ton anhydrite hoppers that worked over the Settle & Carlisle from Long Meg to the chemical works of Widnes. These were built by Ian MacDonald from his own kit.

8. IT'S NOT UNUSUAL

Not an everyday sight – a Class 60 with a train of HTA coal hoppers. This was one of the 'Scunny sets' fitted with screw couplings at each end to allow these locomotives to be used on the Immingham–Scunthorpe circuit instead of the usual Class 66 traction. The date is October 13 2006 and the location is Melton Ross, just east of Barnetby.

Using ready-to-run products, there's always a danger that your locomotives and stock are going to look exactly the same as everyone else's – especially with something as predictable as a privatisation-era coal train. But every now and then there's the opportunity to do something a little different that makes your modelling a bit more interesting. Many HTAs, as a case in point, were covered in graffiti – sometimes brilliantly done, sometimes crude and amateurish. Freightliner's HHAs and GBRf's HYAs were also affected, as indeed is much contemporary rolling stock and railway infrastructure. If you want your trains of coal hoppers to look authentic, there's a wide range of graffiti transfers available in all scales. My preferred brand is Microscale.

9. THE KITS ARE ALRIGHT

Ian Macdonald's kit for the BR 24.5ton coal hopper is a fantastic model that came out a good while before the equally impressive Accurascale ready-to-run version. This is inevitably a risk for kit manufacturers but there'll always be people like me who enjoy building them for their own sake – although whether I fancy building 30-odd of these wagons is another matter. These high-capacity wagons were primarily designed to haul power-station coal and initially at least they worked almost exclusively in long, fixed rakes on circuit diagrams very much like the HOP32AB/HAA wagons that replaced them. Very occasionally they strayed onto other flows, such as coke traffic, but your chances of seeing one in a mixed train – let alone in a local goods yard – were pretty remote.

Hopper wagons need special unloading facilities although at my local rail-served coal yard they'd simply open the bottom doors and dump the load all over the track! In 4mm scale, this 21ton hopper wagon from Mainline – subsequently offered by a variety of manufacturers – is much more the kind of thing you'd see on domestic coal traffic, though it wasn't an especially accurate model. The bodywork is the earlier, riveted pattern whereas the underframe is the later type fitted to all-welded wagons with their very different bodyside bracing. To correct these basic errors I've scraped off all the rivets, built up the side angle from styrene strip and then added detail parts salvaged from various kits. It gives the wagon a very different appearance – these days you can spare yourself the trouble by building the relevant Parkside kits or selecting Hornby's recent ready-to-run hopper based on the LNER design.

10. WEATHERING

Some degree of weathering is pretty well essential for all hopper wagons, reflecting the nature of the payload. The coal hoppers operated by EWS, Freightliner and GBRf soon became pretty filthy and note too the physical damage inflicted on these HTAs making their way out of Barnetby on March 10 2007. That's a challenge to reproduce in model form.

I bulk-weathered the underframes of these Farish 2mm scale HHAs to ensure a measure of consistency throughout the set and then added different shades and nuances to individual wagons. The 4mm scale coke hoppers – each to a different diagram – are from Steam & Things etched brass kits and are in the shabby condition typical of these wagons. Coke and coal are highly corrosive minerals and paintwork is soon attacked by the sulphuric acid that forms when rain falls on the contents of the wagons. Airbrushed and hand-painted rust is augmented by weathering powders, while the BR grey livery is heavily faded.

11. LOADS

The 32 wagons in my rake of first-generation Hornby HAA wagons have additional interior detail as I wanted to be able to run them empty. Not fancying (for now) working up another full set I made removable coal loads so I can run them loaded when required. The basis of these were Parkside Dundas mouldings for the HAA (PA15) on to which I sprinkled the finest coal dust I could find, secured with cheap hairspray and given a prototypically matt finish using Testor's Dullcote.

As an observation, most materials carried in open hopper wagons – coal, aggregates, sand – are a lot finer than many modellers seem to think. The load sits well down inside the wagon, not spilling out over the sides, and each wagon will be loaded the same way with the same number of heaps. As always, study the prototype.

With some hopper designs, removable loads may not be practicable - especially those where the sides slope inwards at a sharp angle such as these Tarmac-operated, Ermewa-leased HOAs. There are plenty of ready-made loads on the market but their 'full to the brim' appearance doesn't always accord with reality. A bit of ingenuity may be called for.

12. REPAIR SHOP

Not all freight operations involve running huge rakes of wagons that the average home layout simply doesn't have room for. Thankfully there are still some revenue-earning services – especially trip workings – that call for modest numbers of vehicles. Meanwhile freight stock of all kinds can often be seen making its way to and from wagon repair facilities, either singly or in short rakes made up of a variety of types.

This Lafarge Tarmac-liveried JGA, seen at Rylstone Quarry in July 2015, has been pulled out of its train to await attention.

Because of its 25mph gearing, a Class 09 shunter was a fixture in the Knottingley/South Milford/Gascoigne Wood area for many years, specifically for dragging 'cripples' to the repair shops at Knottingley. Here on August 2 2007, 09005 gets a move on as it takes a newly repaired HAA wagon back down the busy York-Castleford line at Monk Fryston.

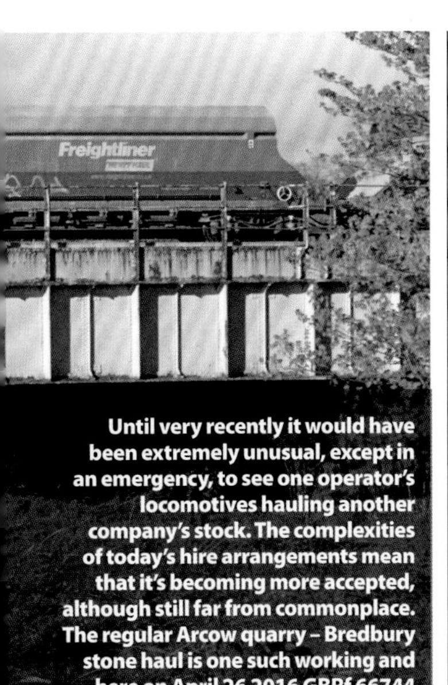

Until very recently it would have been extremely unusual, except in an emergency, to see one operator's locomotives hauling another company's stock. The complexities of today's hire arrangements mean that it's becoming more accepted, although still far from commonplace. The regular Arcow quarry – Bredbury stone haul is one such working and here on April 26 2016 GBRf 66744 *Crossrail* takes a 20-wagon set of Freightliner HIAs over the River Calder at Mirfield.

13. MAKE A DIFFERENCE

To my eye, nothing looks more boring than a long rake of absolutely identical wagons, especially if none of them has been weathered and they all carry the same number. Just study the variety of cement hoppers on view in this typical formation – seven wagons to three different designs. On the 22-wagon train, flat-topped POAs predominated but the presence of the other types makes quite a difference and with Bachmann and Farish offering a variety of ready-to-run cement hoppers this is something you could easily copy.

Cement in powdered form has been transported in hopper wagons for many years. In pre-war days the LMS had some steel-bodied bottom discharge wagons and in the 1950s BR built huge numbers of the distinctive 'Presflo' design. Here, on the East Neuk MRC's impressive 'N' gauge layout Law Junction, a massive and well-varied rake of cement hoppers makes its way north behind the unique Bardon Aggregates-liveried 66623 *Bill Bolsover*.

14. AGGREGATES

Long trains of bogie hoppers have become a common sight in the last 30 years, beginning with the Foster Yeoman and ARC workings from Merehead and Whatley in the Mendips and now radiating outwards from the Peak District (Tunstead, Dowlow, Dove Holes) and Leicestershire quarries (Mountsorrel, Bardon Hill, Croft). Much of the stock is owned by the companies involved, and Bachmann do a splendid JGA hopper in a variety of liveries, with Graham Farish producing the 2mm scale equivalent. The freight companies also have their own dedicated stock that's used on aggregates traffic all over the country, both hopper and box-wagon types.

Yeoman and ARC, of course, owned their own Class 59 fleets but with operators such as Cemex, Lafarge and Tarmac power is contracted in. In heavy rain on January 10 2018, DBC-livered 66130 climbs out of Bury St Edmunds with a Mountsorrel-Barham working consisting of HOA hoppers owned by leasing company Ermewa – an 'N' gauge model is due soon from Revolution trains.

15. TOWARDS THE FUTURE

By far the most impressive – and colourful – hopper trains running on today's network are the long rakes of IIA biomass hoppers serving Drax power station. I got lucky on January 25 2016 when I caught the equally striking 66718 *Sir Peter Hendy OBE* coming along the down slow at Mirfield with biomass hoppers returning to Liverpool Bulk Terminal.

This impressive model of an IIA was produced by Hornby and sold exclusively by Hatton's. Originally intended as a promotional item issued by the Drax Group plc, it has become a sought-after collector's item. Complete sets of 20-odd wagons do exist but you won't find many of them.

GROSV second coming

Hornby Magazine Yearbook No. 9 saw us complete our first big terminus project - Grosvenor Square. Two years later this 'OO' gauge exhibition layout has been expanded and relaunched. It made its maiden outing at the Great Electric Train Show in October 2018. **MIKE WILD** brings the story up to date.

PHOTOGRAPHY, MIKE WILD AND TREVOR JONES

STATISTICS	
Title:	Grosvenor Square
Gauge:	'OO', 16.5mm gauge
Scale:	4mm:1ft
Length:	29ft
Width:	8ft
Track:	Peco code 75, flat bottom rail
Control:	Digital – Gaugemaster and Hornby
Period:	Western Region, 1958-1968

ENOR'S

THE GREAT ELECTRIC TRAIN SHOW OCTOBER 13/14 2018

BUILDING A MODEL RAILWAY against the clock is always a major challenge and at times you have to move the goalposts to make a project achievable. Grosvenor Square fell into that category during its initial build for HM Yearbook No. 9. We had originally planned that the initial phase would consist of a 16ft x 3ft scenic section, to be followed by a storage yard for its debut at the Warley National Model Railway Exhibition in November 2016, but ultimately time got the better of us and rather than create a layout which wasn't complete we reduced its scenic length to 12ft.

As you might expect, this reduction had an effect on its operational potential and meant we had to be clever in the storage yard design to allow it to function as well as was practical while missing a board. That fourth board would have included a full set of inbound junctions allowing the station throat to be operated with two incoming and two outgoing tracks.

Even without the missing board we still put on a show with Grosvenor Square at Warley in 2016 as well as the Great Central Railway Model Event in June 2017 and Spalding Model Railway Exhibition in November 2017. After that though we had no bookings for it in 2018 until the Great Electric Train Show.

With time available while the layout hadn't got bookings we hatched a plan early in the year when planning our projects for 2018 to expand Grosvenor to make it the layout we always intended. We elected to increase its scenic section by 8ft to include the approaching »

1 'Western' D1012 *Western Firebrand* rumbles into Grosvenor Square as a GWR 'King' 4-6-0 departs behind the signalbox. In the carriage sidings a Class 128 DMU waits to enter the station while the depot yard is busy in the background.

2 The Midland Pullman passes the depot on the approach to Grosvenor Square having worked in from the Midland Region on a special. The depot is busy with diesels including classes 22, 40, 43, 46 and 52 while unique BR 'Standard' 71000 *Duke of Gloucester* is being turned on the turntable.

3 Grosvenor Square's scenic section is now 20ft long following addition of the depot scene. The full layout, including storage yard, covers 29ft x 8ft.

junctions, a stretch of four-track main line and a busy motive power depot which could service and turn the locomotives from arriving trains while despatching prepared motive power for departures. We were also keen to put the ADM Turntables turntable into the limelight as part of the layout using the roundhouse scene we built for HM105.

It was a bold plan, particularly as we were also working on expansion of Topley Dale in the first half of the year and also the West Coast Main Line Yearbook project layout, but we could see a slot in the early autumn to make it happen.

24hr challenge

Regular readers will doubtless have seen our feature detailing the expansion of Grosvenor Square in HM136 when we decided to build the extension against the clock in the run up to the Great Electric Train Show. We didn't quite make the timeframe, but by the end of the project we had a fully working 8ft extension.

This time we didn't stick to standard 3ft wide baseboards. Having incorporated the roundhouse scene from our very first 24hr challenge project in the depot scene this dictated the width required to accommodate the four track main line leaving the station as well as the original 2ft 6in width roundhouse board. In total this meant that the new scenic section would widen to 4ft 2in making for a compelling and busy railway scene, all built in 'OO' gauge.

As well as including the roundhouse from a previous challenge, the majority of the Skytrex buildings from our micro layout project (HM117) also migrated across to form the backdrop for Grosvenor's new depot scene while one became part of the foreground. New features included a Ratio coaling tower kit, Faller fuel storage tanks, Bachmann Scenecraft diesel fuelling points, a Kernow/Scenecraft GWR pattern water tower and plenty of Ratio spear and concrete panel fencing to segregate the railway from its surroundings.

Track work continued with Peco code 75 products throughout including two double slips, two large rights, a large left, a curved left and a 'Y' turnout for the new sections together with just over 25 yards of plain track.

Even after completing work for the 24hr challenge there were tasks left to do to make Grosvenor Square fully exhibition ready in its new format which were tackled in the final days before the show. These include final wiring up of the DCC Concepts Cobalt IP digital turnout motors (and addressing them), cleaning and checking of the track including the addition of a couple of power feeds that we had missed out, cutting and fitting of the new fascia panels in 6mm MDF, a modification to the trackplan in the storage yard, painting of the fascia panels and the rear of the backscenes for a consistent appearance and final testing of the turntable now that the full track layout was live. We also had one job left to do on arrival at the show – modification of the trackplan in *RailMaster* which controls points and signals on the scenic section which we ran out of time for in the workshop.

Assembly time

The run-up to any exhibition is always busy even if it is only checking the stock and completing new locomotives or train formations, but when it comes to debuting a modified or new layout it is even more intense. Baseboards have to be packed onto new frames, extra materials are »

Grosvenor on show

From the right Simon Paley, Mike Wild and Philip Sherratt take control of the scenic section's operation at the Great Electric Train Show in October 2018.

Visitors watch as Mike Wild oversees arrival of a BR lined blue 'King' under the control of Simon Paley.

Graham Muspratt (left) **prepares for the next departure to the storage yard while Mark Chivers** (right) **turns a 'Warship' on the turntable.**

BRCW prototype D0260 *Lion* always captures attention as it arrives at Grosvenor Square.

carried, just in case, and there are always little details that you think of while packing the van.

We had tested the new section prior to the show, but only independently with one of the original boards at each end. This meant that we knew trains would run through it and that everything worked electrically, but equally that it had never been run as a complete layout. That was all to do during the Friday setup at the Great Electric Train Show on October 12.

Having prepared the floorplan and accommodated all 83 stands which made up the show we then turned our attention to assembling Grosvenor Square. The original station boards followed our well practiced routine and were soon followed by the new boards, all of which went together quickly and without any dramas. The storage yard was then assembled bringing the complete 29ft x 8ft layout together in a little over an hour for the first time. Now though we had the tasks of fitting all the connecting cables, arranging the control bus from the Gaugemaster Prodigy base station, connecting two computers, two Hornby Elites and the ADM Turntables controller into the layout. This all takes time and while one of us was occupied with that process others were cleaning track, laying out buildings, adding road vehicles and making final checks for baseboard alignment.

We now had a fully assembled layout and the opportunity to modify the trackplan for the scenic section in RailMaster to accommodate the additional nine point motors which it would control. This was quickly carried out and once drawn the points were tested, their throw direction corrected on RailMaster where necessary and everything was ready for the first train movements.

We rarely fully stock the layout on a Friday night at shows and the Great Electric Train Show was no exception. A handful of train movements took place checking that trains would run throughout the entire layout and that they negotiated the complex return loop storage yard which has three Gaugemaster return loop modules installed to allow trains to continue uninterrupted through the storage yard under digital control.

Come Saturday morning and the baseboards had settled into their new environment overnight. A few adjustments were made to their levels and then the process of putting together all the trains took place to give us a rake of six-coach formations for main line expresses – the longest the platforms can currently hold. Final checks with the turntable were made too and a selection of locomotives was laid out in the depot ready to fund arriving trains.

4 Churchward '47XX' 2-8-0 4706 coasts under the road bridge and passes a Collett 'Grange' 4-6-0 departing with a stopping train. The background is dominated by the depot.

Learning on the job

Being its first operating session in its new format we all had plenty to learn on Saturday morning and with six operators taking to the controls we were aiming to keep the railway busy and entertaining for the visiting public. One took on the main scenic section control with two supporting drivers while another was in charge of the storage yard control panel with a driver to hand too. The sixth operator was solely in charge of moving locomotives through the depot and turning them on the turntable to prepare them for the next departures.

The railway ran well and we soon had the hang of how it operated and what it was capable of. We did realise during the first day that we needed more locomotives available on shed and a better system as we ran out of spare locomotives on the scenic section on occasions during the Saturday, particularly those which were suitable for the train type that was waiting in the station. As a result we organised the depot on Sunday to have two arrival roads – one for steam locomotives which passed over the ashpit and under the coaling tower and one for diesels which avoided those facilities. Locomotives which had been turned were separated into express and mixed traffic types meaning that it was now simpler to get the right locomotive for the right train.

Keen observers noted that we were turning steam and diesel locomotives during the weekend with the latter being to suit model railway operation as they only have couplings fitted at one end to allow full bufferbeam pipework to be fitted at the other. If nothing else it meant we got to use the ADM turntable more during the weekend.

Having established these new patterns of

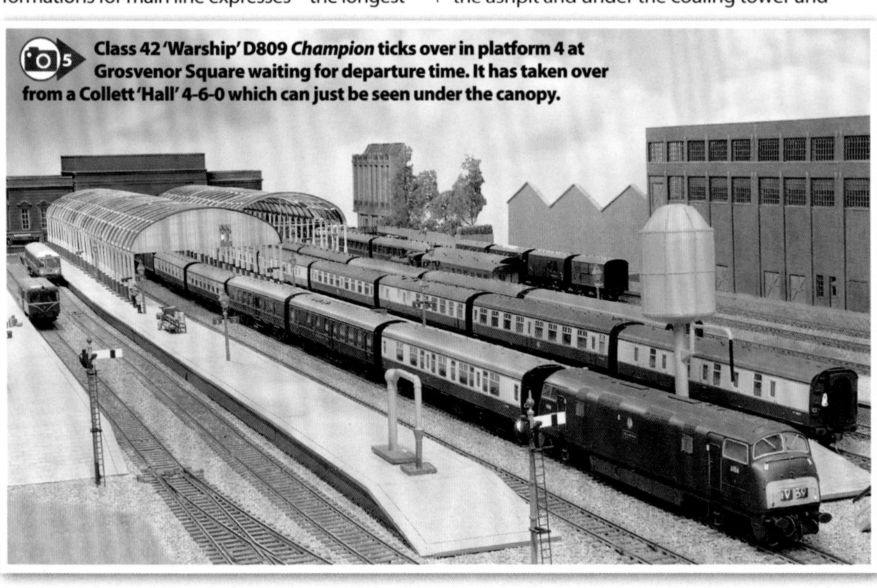

5 Class 42 'Warship' D809 *Champion* ticks over in platform 4 at Grosvenor Square waiting for departure time. It has taken over from a Collett 'Hall' 4-6-0 which can just be seen under the canopy.

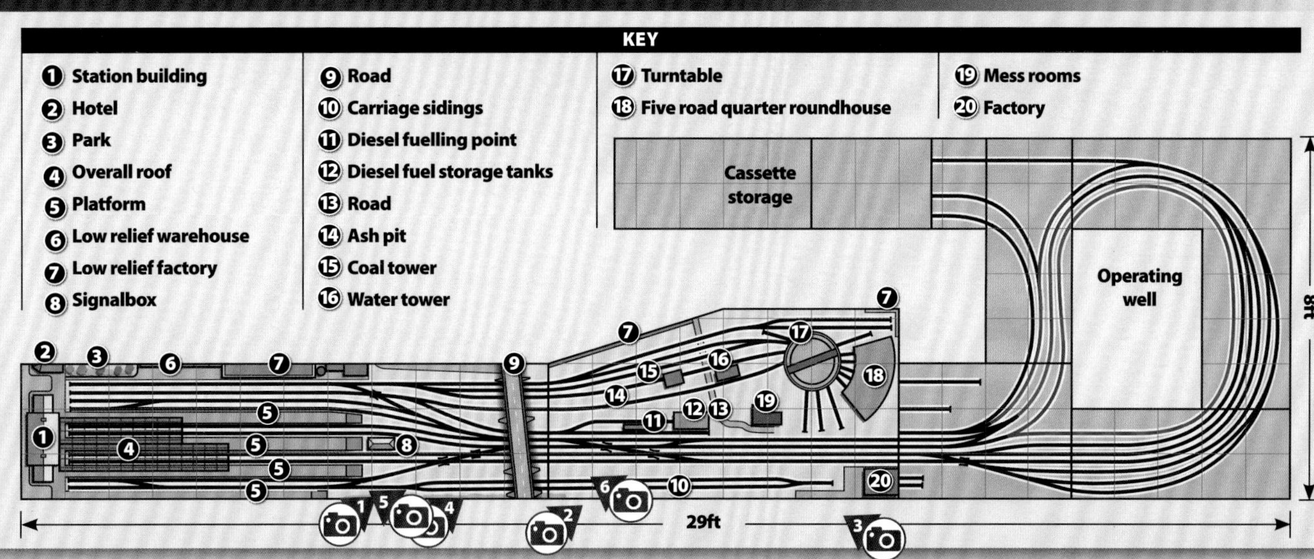

operation the layout settled down into a rhythm on Sunday and we were even able to pre-empt arriving trains by bringing locomotives out from the depot earlier in the process which helped to keep the railway operation going with fewer spells when there was only limited activity. The changes to the arrival and departure roads in the depot assisted this too.

Even with a full crew of six operators running the layout there were still areas of the layout that went virtually unused including the sidings behind the station and the parcels loop at the front. Still, we can see the potential for the layout's next outing at the Basingstoke Model Railway Exhibition in March 2019.

Next steps

Grosvenor Square is now safely stored again for winter and in that time we will be making further amendments, adjustments and embellishments to the locomotive fleet including weathering, coupling adjustment and further detailing. There are several steam locomotives which are without crews while, as you might expect, there are also new locomotives we want to add to the roster that we just didn't have time to complete. The layout too will benefit from further upgrades in 2019 including, we hope, bracket signals and ground signals, wiring up of the yard lights, repairing of the wiring for the depot buildings and more enhancement of the depot area with figures and detailing.

Its first show in its extended format was a great success and despite one or two teething troubles it ran smoothly and reliably throughout the weekend and we are looking forward to being back out in public with it again. We already have plans for further extensions – we'd really like to make the platforms 2ft longer – but for the short term Grosvenor will be operated in its current format. As well as the Basingstoke exhibition in March it is also set to attend the Great Central Railway Model Event in June 2019 and full details of both of these shows will be published in future issues of *Hornby Magazine*. ■

6 A GWR 'King' 4-6-0 departs Grosvenor Square under the road bridge at the station throat – an image that wasn't possible until extension of the layout.

'NIGHT OWL' *makeover*

Heljan's GWR '47XX' 2-8-0 touched down in mid-2018 offering a new choice of 2-8-0 for fast freights on the Western Region. **MIKE WILD** shows how the model can be equipped with a digital sound decoder while giving it a 'lived in' look at the same time.

THE CHURCHWARD '47XX' 2-8-0s were great looking locomotives. Just nine were built between 1919 and 1923 and sightings in daylight were rare as the class was designed to handle overnight fast vacuum-fitted freight work. As time progressed their duties expanded and by the British Railways era they were regulars on Summer Saturday relief trains and parcels work too.

Their traditional nocturnal operations brought the nickname 'Night Owls' to the '47XXs' and while none were preserved the Great Western Society is currently building a new example of these impressive and large 2-8-0s at Didcot Railway Centre.

Heljan's model of the 'Night Owl' has been eagerly awaited by Great Western Railway and Western Region modellers as it adds something quite different to the range of ready-to-run motive power. It might have the typical family appearance of a Churchward locomotive, but these 2-8-0s will always stand out from the crowd. The model has been released in GWR and BR liveries with our example being 4706 in BR black with early crests on the tender sides.

Like all of its steam locomotives, the Heljan 2-8-0 has a locomotive mounted motor and drive system with the decoder and speaker space positioned in the tender. On paper the '47XX' should be a straightforward sound conversion – and in fact if you choose a LokSound decoder it is, as these decoders come with a speaker connected to the

SOUND FUNCTIONS	
F0	Lights on/off
F1	Sound on/off
F2	Whistle
F3	Short whistle
F4	Guard's whistle
F5	Safety valves
F6	Coal shovelling
F7	Watering
F8	Aux 2 (brown wire for smoke generator)
F9	Flange squeal
F10	Injector

decoder by wires. However, other brands – including the Zimo MX644D we selected – don't come with speakers connected from the factory and Heljan hasn't provided a readily usable connection point for these instances. There is a spare socket, although no plug is included, and nor are instructions for its use, so to connect a speaker in our project meant soldering it to the bottom of the pins on the 21-pin plug on the circuit board. This is a delicate operation which will require a fine soldering iron nib, but it is perfectly achievable.

To make the most of the MX644D we also connected a 'stay alive' capacitor as detailed in the instruction sheet with the decoder. The decoder has inbuilt circuits to charge and use the stored power from the capacitor while the 'stay alive' system will keep the sound on through brief interruptions in power delivery and help prevent stalling at slow speeds.

The Heljan '47XX' is a good looking model and one which is sure to have been popular on GWR and WR period layouts since its introduction – adding sound and weathering, as we have here, just makes it even better.

The step by step guide explains the full installation process for the Heljan GWR '47XX' 2-8-0 making it ready to make the right noises at the head of parcels and fast freights. ■

TOOLS

- » Crosshead screwdriver
- » Solder
- » Soldering iron
- » Wire strippers
- » Insulation tape
- » Scissors
- » Heatshrink tubing

WHAT WE USED

PRODUCT	MANUFACTURER	CAT NO.
GWR 'Hall' sound file	Digitrains	ZS012
MX644D 21-pin sound decoder	Zimo	MX644D
10mm x 15mm cube speaker	Zimo	LS10x15
Decoder wire, black	TCS	1216

TECHNICAL DETAILS

Manufacturer:	*www.hornby.com*
First released:	2018 (HM132)
Cat No (featured):	4783
Current alternatives:	4780-4785
Description:	GWR Churchward '47XX' 2-8-0
Gauge:	'OO'/16.5mm
Scale:	4mm:1ft
Length (over buffers):	268mm
Price:	£199.95
Era:	3-5
Couplings:	NEM pockets with small tension locks
DCC:	DCC ready, 21-pin socket
Speaker space:	23mm round in tender
Exterior lights:	None
Interior lights:	None
Motor type:	Five pole, can motor
Flywheel:	One
Wheel arrangement:	2-8-0
Purpose:	Mixed traffic
Haulage capacity (expected):	10 carriages
Haulage capacity (actual):	10+ carriages

Heljan's GWR '47XX' 2-8-0 was released in May 2018 (HM132) and has been made available in GWR and BR colour schemes. 4706 departs heading a long fitted freight replicating a typical formation for the class in the early 1950s. It has been weathered with Lifecolor acrylics.

STEP BY STEP INSTALLING DIGITAL SOUND IN A HELJAN GWR '47XX' 2-8-0 IN 'OO'

1 This sound project begins with Heljan's model of the '47XX' 2-8-0, a choice of speakers and a Zimo MX644D decoder loaded with 'Hall' sounds from Digitrains. The sound file was selected for its GWR character and the exhaust beat will be adjusted to match the 2-8-0's wheel size.

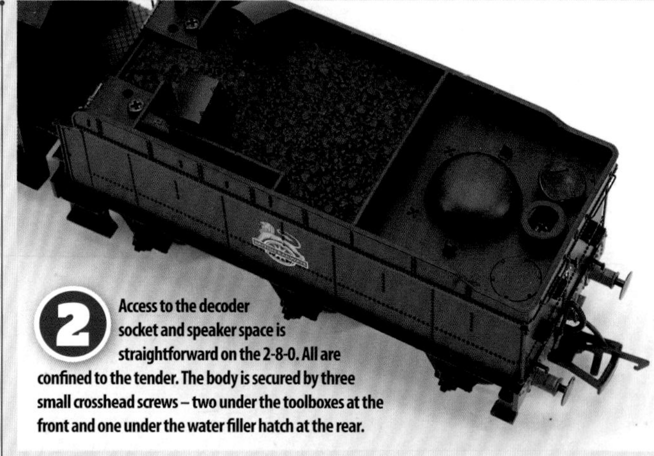

2 Access to the decoder socket and speaker space is straightforward on the 2-8-0. All are confined to the tender. The body is secured by three small crosshead screws – two under the toolboxes at the front and one under the water filler hatch at the rear.

3 With the body removed the decoder socket is immediately obvious on top of the green circuit board. We had already fitted this model with a Gaugemaster DCC27 Omni decoder for testing purposes. The speaker space is at the rear of the tender at the bottom of the weight.

4 The main Printed Circuit Board (PCB) is only held in place with double-sided tape and it is easier to remove it from the tender to disconnect and connect a decoder. The Zimo MX644D decoder fits straight onto the pins, as would a LokSound 21-pin sound decoder.

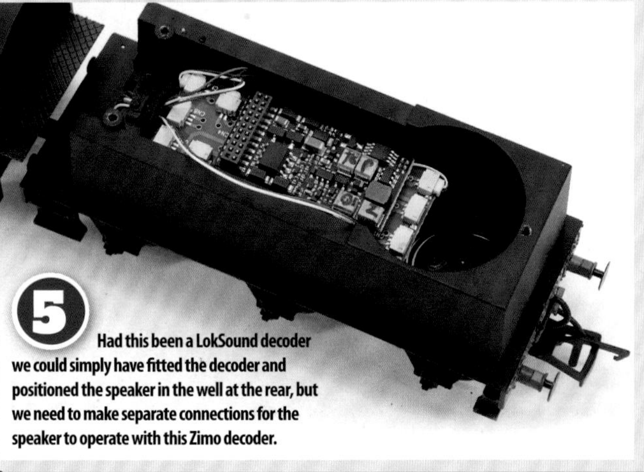

5 Had this been a LokSound decoder we could simply have fitted the decoder and positioned the speaker in the well at the rear, but we need to make separate connections for the speaker to operate with this Zimo decoder.

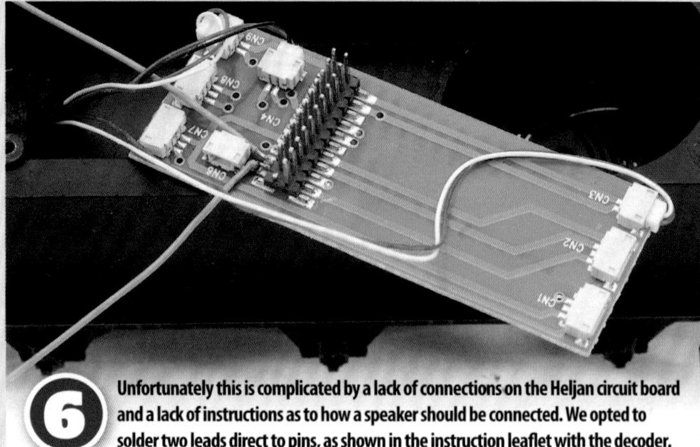

6 Unfortunately this is complicated by a lack of connections on the Heljan circuit board and a lack of instructions as to how a speaker should be connected. We opted to solder two leads direct to pins, as shown in the instruction leaflet with the decoder. You will need a fine 1mm soldering iron nib for this and a steady hand.

7 A great advantage of the Zimo MX644D (and 8-pin MX645R equivalent) is the built-in circuit to support a 'stay alive' capacitor. To connect a capacitor, two leads need to be soldered to the two solder pads on the underside of the decoder. Keep the instructions to hand, as positive and negative must be correctly connected to the capacitor.

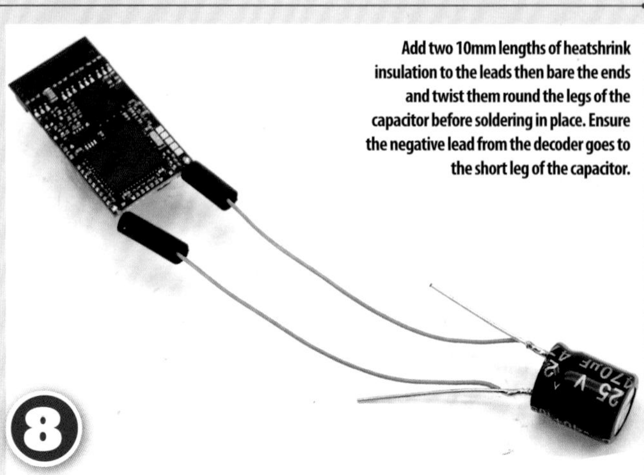

8 Add two 10mm lengths of heatshrink insulation to the leads then bare the ends and twist them round the legs of the capacitor before soldering in place. Ensure the negative lead from the decoder goes to the short leg of the capacitor.

Churchward '47XX' 2-8-0 4707 approaches Bathampton Junction with a lengthy freight for the Westbury route on September 15 1962. Hugh Ballantyne/Railphotoprints.uk.

9 The heatshrink insulation is then moved over the soldered connections and reduced in size with the side of a soldering iron to complete this stage of the project.

10 To allow the capacitor to fit into the speaker well along with a speaker we chose a Zimo 10mm x 15mm cube speaker. This has been soldered to the pair of leads connected to the pins on the decoder plug in step 6.

11 Everything is then test fitted into the tender before being fixed in place. We have also covered the metal surface and connections on the speaker with black insulation tape to prevent any short circuits.

12 The tender body can then be refitted taking care to ensure that none of the wires snag during reassembly. Use the original screws to secure the tender body in place.

STEP BY STEP INSTALLING DIGITAL SOUND IN A HELJAN GWR '47XX' 2-8-0 IN 'OO'

13 To enhance the '47XX' further we wanted to give it a lightly weathered finish – nothing too dramatic, as these 2-8-0s were generally kept in fairly smart external condition. The starting point is a dusting of Lifecolor Frame Dirt (UA719) across the underframe from an airbrush. We used a business card as a mask to contain the spray in the right areas.

14

The same colour was also applied around the edges of the coal space – we aren't worried about overspray onto the coal at this point as a real coal load will be added later.

15

Next, Lifecolor Burned Black (UA736) was sprayed over the boiler barrel, cabsides and tender to tone the factory satin sheen down. Again, nothing too heavy, just a light dusting to make it look like a working locomotive.

USEFUL LINKS	
Heljan	*www.heljan.com*
Digitrains	*www.digitrains.co.uk*
Zimo	*www.zimo-digital.co.uk*
Lifecolor paints	*www.airbrushes.com*

16 To differentiate the smokebox from the boiler – and representing the extra heat transferred to this area – Lifecolor Worn Black (UA734) was used for this section. The numberplate and shedplate were given a wipe over before the paint had dried. The cab roof was painted with the same colour.

Beginner SKILL LEVEL Intermediate Advanced

Subtle weathering with Lifecolor acrylics breathes more life into Heljan's imposing model of the '47XX' 2-8-0.

17 Completing the boiler is a streak of Black Smoke Tensocrom from the Lifecolor range to represent exhaust stains along the top of the locomotive. It's a very subtle colour, but one which adds more tones to the overall finish.

18 The finishing touches on the buffers are Lifecolor Dirty Grease Effect (UA262) applied by brush to reflect grease on the buffer heads.

19 The motion has been brushed over with Lifecolor Grease Effect (UA263), ensuring that the moving parts can still rotate or slide freely.

20 Completing the model is a pair of lamps for a Class 4 train – parcels or fast fitted freight and a real coal load in the tender. The latter is secured in place with PVA glue brushed over the factory moulded load.

Review of the Year 2017-2018

2018 has proved to be an exciting year with plenty of new models and a new manufacturer entering the fold. **MARK CHIVERS** looks back over the highlights of the past year's newly-tooled locomotives and rolling stock across 'OO', 'N', 'O' and 'OO9'.

ANOTHER YEAR HAS PASSED, and a busy one at that, with more than 50 all-new ready-to-run models appearing across 'OO', 'N', 'OO9' and 'O' gauge.

Given the sheer number of new projects hitting the shelves as well as the re-liveries and re-runs of previously released models, it truly has been an outstanding year for modellers in all scales.

Interestingly, Bachmann, Dapol, Heljan, Hornby and Oxford Rail accounted for just over 30 of the year's newly-tooled releases, while the remaining 20 new projects were independent/retailer commissions. The year also witnessed the appearance of a new ready-to-run manufacturer on the scene, Accurascale, which debuted its first 'OO' gauge wagon with the HOP24/HUO 24.5ton coal hoppers. This was followed up with the announcement of further models including an 'O' gauge HOP24/HUO and 'OO' gauge APCM Cemflo/PCV powder cement wagons and PCA bulk cement wagons, with more promised.

But this year, all-new releases weren't limited purely to the major scales, as Bachmann also delivered the first of its 'OO9' products with a new locomotive and two wagons appearing complementing the off-the-shelf models and kits already offered by other manufacturers.

Dapol impressed with the running characteristics and detail of its new 'OO' gauge Adams 'B4' 0-4-0T.

As a follow up to its Class 122 Dapol released the Pressed Steel Class 121 for 'OO' gauge in December 2017.

Locomotives

Every year manufacturers strive to add a good selection of motive power to suit all interests, but this year 'OO' gauge Southern modellers appear to have benefitted most, to the tune of six new locomotives, with Bachmann's London, Brighton & South Coast Railway (LBSCR) Billinton 'H2' 4-4-2, Dapol's Adams 'B4' 0-4-0T, Hatton's South Eastern & Chatham Railway (SECR) 'P' 0-6-0T, Hornby's Wainwright 'H' Class 0-4-4T and OO Works' Drummond 'D15' 4-4-0 for steam era modellers plus Heljan's Class 07 0-6-0 diesel-electric shunter, a type synonymous with operations in and around Southampton Docks in the 1960s and 1970s.

The Great Western Railway (GWR) wasn't forgotten, as Heljan's 'OO' GWR '47XX' 2-8-0 arrived during April, the 'Night Owl' appearing well-detailed and proving powerful whilst hauling a load of 30+ wagons with ease, on test. Meanwhile, Locomotion Models' long-awaited 'OO' gauge model of the Great Northern Railway (GNR) Stirling 'single' 4-2-2 appeared in July. This model was manufactured by Rapido Trains of Canada and benefitted from being laser-scanned using the National Collection prototype on display at Locomotion in Shildon. The attention to detail and appearance of this model didn't go unnoticed, as readers' votes gained it the *Hornby Magazine* Model Railway Award for 'Best 'OO' gauge locomotive' during a presentation at the Great Electric Train Show in October.

Given the previous year's focus on compact »

Hornby's Class 800 five-car unit debuted in GWR green for 'OO' gauge in March 2018. More are due before the end of the year.

motive power and industrial prototypes, just one 'OO' gauge industrial locomotive appeared this time round with Hatton's delightful Andrew Barclay 0-4-0ST debuting during April. Detail differences between the 14in and 16in cylinder locomotives were faithfully reproduced including larger tanks, additional framing, window styling, buffer sizes and more.

Shortly after *Hornby Magazine's Yearbook No. 10* closed for press, Hornby's all-new Stanier 'Duchess' 4-6-2 appeared with retailers and proved so popular that the manufacturer arranged a re-run of 46256 *Sir William Stanier F.R.S.* in BR lined maroon to satisfy demand, Dapol issued its 'OO' gauge GWR streamlined railcar, displaying the stylish complex curves of the prototype well, while at the other end of the era spectrum, Hornby released its ultra-modern model of the Class 800 InterCity Express Train (IET) during February. Initially available in modern GWR livery, it was also accompanied by a special limited edition two-vehicle pack containing power cars in Hitachi test train colours.

Dapol maintained its momentum by following up its 'OO' Class 122 diesel railcar with the Pressed Steel Class 121 variant in December, issuing standard models in BR green with 'speed whiskers', BR green with small yellow warning panels, BR blue and BR blue/grey examples, together with limited editions in BR GW150 chocolate and cream, BR Network SouthEast, Arriva Trains Wales, Railtrack blue/green, Railtrack maroon, Chiltern Railways blue and Chiltern Railways green with small yellow warning panels.

Kernow Model Rail Centre took delivery of its third version of the Bulleid 1-Co-Co-1 diesel, 10203, for 'OO' in July, complete with prototypical detail differences, while Bachmann issued its Class 70/8 Co-Co diesel in Colas Railfreight and

In 'O' gauge Heljan released its second version of the Class 20 modelling the later centre headcode locomotives.

Dapol's original streamlined GWR railcar made its debut for 'OO' in November 2017.

The Gloucester Class 128 parcels railcar was upscaled to 'O' by Heljan.

Freightliner colours, reflecting the later air intake and bodyside modifications. Completing the line-up for this year's 'OO' gauge diesels and electrics was Hornby's much-anticipated Class 87 Bo-Bo, which touched down in September with two versions offered in BR blue and InterCity colour schemes. A Virgin Trains liveried example is expected in 2019.

Manufacture of 'N' gauge projects was a little slow again this year with three newly-tooled locomotives making it to market, including Bachmann's Graham Farish Class 40 1-Co-Co-1 diesel as the last *Hornby Magazine* Yearbook closed for press and Dapol's Class 68 Bo-Bo diesel during March. Both models certainly looked the part with plenty of exquisite detailing and exceptional running characteristics.

Staying with the contemporary railway scene, Revolution Trains also released its long-awaited 'N' gauge Class 390 Pendolino Electric Multiple Unit (EMU) to crowd-funders who had supported the project from the start. Originally launched in 2014, the Pendolino was another model to be manufactured by Rapido Trains, with superb decoration and exquisite detailing, with various train lengths available up to the full 11-car versions. Voting for all three models in the *Hornby Magazine* Model Railway Awards proved popular, with Bachmann's Class 40 taking the title of 'Best 'N' gauge locomotive'.

Hatton's ticked off the sought after ICI bogie hoppers for 'OO' gauge in spring 2018. Diamond and plate frame bogies were offered with the latest releases being factory weathered editions.

While Bachmann may have been a little quieter this year on the locomotive front in 'OO' and 'N', the manufacturer concentrated efforts on its fledgling 'OO9' range with the release of its eagerly-awaited Baldwin 10-12-D 4-6-0T in March. Three versions formed the initial batch in weathered black as preserved at the Leighton Buzzard Railway, Ashover lined maroon and Glyn Valley Tramway lined black. To accompany the locomotives, Bachmann had also issued its first 'OO9' bogie goods vans and D class open wagons »

Bachmann delivered its Brighton 'H2' 4-4-2 for 'OO' gauge including this BR liveried example as 32424 *Beachy Head* – the last in service with BR's Southern Region.

a few months earlier in November 2017.

Modellers in 'O' gauge received a boost, with six new locomotives from Dapol, Heljan and Minerva Model Railways. Dapol introduced its 'O' gauge LMS 'Jinty' 0-6-0T just as *Hornby Magazine's* Yearbook No.10 closed for press, with versions issued with and without running numbers and factory-fitted sound options too. GWR modellers found themselves with a choice of 'O' gauge '57XX' 0-6-0PT models from Dapol and Minerva Model Railways, while Dapol also re-issued the former Lionheart '64XX'/'74XX' variants together with the complementary ex-Lionheart GWR autocoach, paving the way for a potential flurry of 'O' gauge GWR branch lines. Dapol's model of the '57XX' 0-6-0PT also secured readers' votes for the *Hornby Magazine* Model Railway Awards' "Best 'O' gauge locomotive' category. That's not the end of it, though, as Heljan added to the Great Western motive power roster with the arrival of its first 'O' gauge ready-to-run steam locomotive, the GWR '61XX' 2-6-2T, during September.

Diesel-era modellers weren't forgotten, as Heljan delivered its centre headcode Class 20 Bo-Bo diesel and Class 128 Diesel Parcels Unit at the turn of 2018, with its Class 25/3 Bo-Bo diesel expected within days of this issue of the Yearbook closing for press.

Carriages

One of the highlights of the year was the arrival of Rails of Sheffield's exquisite limited edition 'OO' gauge model of the London and North Eastern Railway (LNER) Dynamometer Car. This impressive and much sought-after model took the benchmark for carriages to a whole new level with a high level of detail inside and out. The complex LNER teak livery was well-executed, interior illumination proved novel and its stunning detailing guaranteed its *Hornby Magazine* Model Railway Award as 'Best 'OO' gauge carriage/wagon'.

Hornby added a 'OO' gauge Maunsell 59ft

Great Western Railway steam designs were in focus for 'O' gauge with Heljan delivering its '61XX' 2-6-2T while Dapol and Minerva produced 0-6-0PTs for the scale.

Accurascale delivered its first British outline ready-to-run wagon in 'OO' gauge – the BR 24.5ton HUO hopper.

Revolution Trains produced its first transition era crowd-funded model for 'N' gauge – the Class B 35ton four-wheel tanker.

In 'N' gauge Revolution Trains showed the power of crowd-funding with its full length models of the Class 390 Pendolino.

Brand new Mk 2f carriages were released by Bachmann for 'OO' gauge in October 2018.

Restaurant Car to its range in July, filling a large catering gap for Southern modellers and enabling more authentic rakes of vehicles to be formed. Flush-glazed, it also featured pre-printed curtains and excellent body and roof detailing. Meanwhile, Oxford Rail drip-fed its new range of 'OO' gauge BR Mk 3a locomotive hauled carriages to market with First Open (FO), Standard Open (SO) and Restaurant Buffet (RFB/RUB) variants made available across the year in InterCity and BR blue/grey colours.

During September, the first of Bachmann's long-awaited 'OO' gauge BR Mk 2f air-conditioned carriages began to appear with examples including FO and RFB vehicles, while Tourist Standard Opens (TSO) and Brake Standard Opens (BSO) were also due imminently. Also due at the same time were Bachmann's BR Mk 2f Driving Brake Standard Opens (DBSO) in BR blue/grey and ScotRail liveries. Impressively detailed inside and out, most are available in standard DC and DCC onboard formats - the latter featuring interior lighting options which also includes working tail lights and Central Door Locking (CDL) lights, where fitted.

Newly-tooled 'N' gauge coaches were few and far between during the year, with Dapol adding the Southern Railway Maunsell four-compartment brake carriages to its range, appearing in sets during June. Such was their popularity, they received the *Hornby Magazine* Model Railway Award for 'Best 'N' gauge carriage/ wagon'. And so it turns out, the same can be said for 'O' gauge modellers who voted for Darstaed/ Ellis Clark Trains' new BR Mk 1 carriages as the 'Best 'O' gauge carriage/wagon' in the *Hornby* »

Hornby released its West Coast Main Line Class 87 overhead electric for 'OO' in September as both 87035 *Robert Burns* in BR blue and 87010 *King Arthur* in InterCity colours.

Dapol started its 'O' gauge releases for our review with the LMS Fowler 'Jinty' 0-6-0T. The model was released in LMS black, BR black and Somerset and Dorset Joint Railway blue as illustrated here.

Depot and snow scenes will benefit from Hatton's 2018 model of the Beilhack snowplough for 'OO'.

Hatton's produced its compact Andrew Barclay 0-4-0ST in a mixture of colour schemes for 'OO' gauge as well as producing both 14in and 16in locomotives.

Magazine Model Railway Awards. Featuring fine etched brass sides, sprung metal buffers, detailed interiors, metal underframe, interior illumination and more, they are available as BR Mk 1 Corridor First (FK), Tourist Standard Open (TSO), Brake Corridor Composite (BCK), Brake Corridor Standard (BSK), plus catering vehicles in a choice of liveries.

Wagons

One much-requested model through the years finally arrived during February when Hatton's took delivery of its exclusive 'OO' gauge ICI hopper wagons. Manufactured by Oxford Rail, eight variants were produced in pristine and weathered finishes, covering their whole lifespan and fitted with either diamond or plate frame bogies. For something a little different, Hatton's also released its Beilhack ZZA Snowplough during May with a good selection of variants in BR, Network SouthEast, Railtrack and Network Rail liveries. Utilising Class 40 and Class 45 bogies, detail differences included the solar panels fitted to some Railtrack liveried examples.

Kernow Model Rail Centre issued its 'OO' gauge models of the YCV 34ton 'Turbot' spoil wagons during February, with four in civil engineers 'Dutch' livery and four in EWS livery. Each carried individual running numbers, together with variation of printed details between wagons. Incidentally, Dapol has confirmed that its 'OO' gauge model of the 'Turbot' is also due to be released before the year end.

As previously mentioned, Accurascale launched during the year. The team behind the venture also run Irish Railway Models, whose release of the CIE 'Bubble' cement tank wagons caught our attention in December. Accurascale's first British outline 'OO' gauge model was the HUO 24.5ton hopper wagon which appeared in May, available singly and in triple packs of individually numbered models. Total Operations Processing System (TOPS) and Pre-TOPS models were offered. Subsequently, an 'O' gauge model was announced with further 'OO' wagons planned.

By late summer, Bachmann had caught up on some of its wagon projects, delivering TMC's exclusive 22ton double-bolster/plate wagons during August, with single and twin packs available covering bolster wagons, reach wagons, barrier vehicles and the like. For general release, Bachmann released its 'OO' gauge BR Mk 1 63ft Carflats in BR bauxite and BR Motorail blue, adding even more variety to its range of Mk 1 rolling stock, while its FFA/FGA Freightliner flat wagons are due imminently too.

Arriving just before this issue closed for press, the first of Hornby's 'OO' gauge LNER 20ton 'Toad E' brake vans arrived with retailers during October in BR grey, finished as E175712 (Cat No. R6834). Further examples in BR grey and LNER bauxite are also expected.

In terms of general release 'N' gauge wagons, Bachmann re-issued its Conflat with a newly-tooled BA container in late 2017, providing more variety in the process, while modern-era 'N' gauge modellers were treated to the release of Dapol's MJA twin bogie box wagons, available in Freightliner green and the latest GB Railfreight blue colour scheme, widening the operating sphere of these vehicles.

Commissions and crowd-funded models during the year included the N Gauge Society's (NGS) new 'N' gauge BR Mk 1 63ft Carflats. These were commissioned from Bachmann exclusively for members of the NGS with six models produced covering BR brown, BR bauxite, BR Motorail blue and Railease yellow with BR1 and B4 bogie variants. Meanwhile, Revolution Trains added to its crowd-funded portfolio with two more completed 'N' gauge wagon projects - its 35ton Class B tank wagons during June and the IZA Cargowaggon twin vans in October.

Finally, with the upsurge of interest in 'O' gauge, four newly-tooled wagon projects came

Oxford Rail launched its new range of locomotive hauled Mk 3 rolling stock in BR blue and grey and InterCity liveries for 'OO' in 2018.

Dapol's new model of the YCV 'Turbot' spoil wagon for 'OO' was due to arrive imminently as this Yearbook closed for press.

TABLE 1 – 2017-2018 NEW READY-TO-RUN PRODUCTS

MODEL	SCALE	MANUFACTURER	RELEASED	FEATURED
Wainwright 'H' Class 0-4-4T	'OO'	Hornby	October 2017	HM126
Drummond 'D15' 4-4-0	'OO'	OO Works	October 2017	HM126
LMS 'Jinty' 0-6-0T	'O'	Dapol	October 2017	HM126
Conflat with BA container	'N'	Graham Farish	October 2017	HM126
GWR streamlined railcar	'OO'	Dapol	November 2017	HM127
Bogie goods van	'009'	Bachmann	November 2017	HM127
D class open wagon	'009'	Bachmann	November 2017	HM127
GWR 'Iron Mink' box van	'O'	Minerva Model Railways	November 2017	HM127
Class 121 Diesel Railcar	'OO'	Dapol	December 2017	HM128
CIE 'Bubble' cement tank wagons	'OO'	Irish Railway Models	December 2017	HM128
Class 800 InterCity Express Train	'OO'	Hornby	February 2018	HM129
YCV 34ton 'Turbot' spoil wagon	'OO'	Kernow Model Rail Centre	February 2018	
SECR 'P' Class 0-6-0T	'OO'	Hatton's	January 2018	HM129
Class 20 Bo-Bo diesel	'O'	Heljan	January 2018	HM129
50ton bogie 'Warwell' well wagon	'O'	Heljan	January 2018	HM129
Class 128 Diesel Parcels Units	'O'	Heljan	January 2018	HM129
Andrew Barclay 0-4-0ST	'OO'	Hatton's	April 2018	HM130
BR Mk 1 63ft Carflat	'N'	N Gauge Society	February 2018	HM130
ICI bogie hopper wagons	'OO'	Hatton's	February 2018	HM130
BR Mk 3a carriages	'OO'	Oxford Rail	February 2018	HM130
Class 390 Pendolino EMU	'N'	Revolution Trains	February 2018	HM130
BR Mk 1 carriages	'O'	Darstaed	February 2018	HM130
GWR '57XX' 0-6-0PT	'O'	Dapol	March 2018	HM131
Baldwin 10-12-D 4-6-0T	'009'	Bachmann	March 2018	HM131
Class 68 Bo-Bo diesel	'N'	Dapol	March 2018	HM131
Class 87 Bo-Bo electric	'OO'	Hornby	September 2018	HM132
GWR 7ton Gunpowder van	'O'	Minerva Model Railways	April 2018	HM132
GWR '47XX' 2-8-0	'OO'	Heljan	April 2018	HM132
Beilhack ZZA snowplough	'OO'	Hatton's	May 2018	HM132
Class 70/8 Co-Co diesel	'OO'	Bachmann	June 2018	HM132
GNR Stirling 'single' 4-2-2	'OO'	Locomotion Models	July 2018	HM133
Adams 'B4' 0-4-0T	'OO'	Dapol	June 2018	HM134
Class 07 0-6-0 diesel shunter	'OO'	Heljan	June 2018	HM134
Maunsell 59ft Restaurant Car	'OO'	Hornby	June 2018	HM134
HUO 24.5ton hopper wagon	'OO'	Accurascale	May 2018	HM134
35ton Class B tank wagons	'N'	Revolution Trains	June 2018	HM134
Maunsell four-compartment brake	'N'	Dapol	June 2018	HM134
MJA twinset bogie box wagons	'N'	Dapol	June 2018	HM134
Bulleid 1-Co-Co-1 diesel (10203)	'OO'	Kernow Model Rail Centre	July 2018	HM135
LNER Dynamometer Car	'OO'	Rails of Sheffield	July 2018	HM135
GWR '57XX' 0-6-0PT	'O'	Minerva Model Railways	July 2018	HM135
22ton double-bolster/plate wagons	'OO'	The Model Centre (TMC)	August 2018	HM135
LBSCR 'H2' 4-4-2	'OO'	Bachmann	September 2018	HM136
BR Mk 1 63ft Carflat	'OO'	Bachmann	September 2018	HM136
YCV 34ton 'Turbot' spoil wagon	'OO'	Dapol	October 2018*	HM136
GWR '61XX' 2-6-2T	'O'	Heljan	September 2018	HM137
BR Mk 2f coaches	'OO'	Bachmann	September 2018	HM137
FFA/FGA Freightliner flat wagons	'OO'	Bachmann	October 2018*	HM137
LNER 20ton 'Toad E' brake van	'OO'	Hornby	October 2018	HM138
BR 20ton brake van	'O'	Dapol	October 2018	HM138
IZA Cargowaggon twin vans	'N'	Revolution Trains	October 2018	HM138

*** Expected arrival date at the time of closing for press.**

to fruition during the year with the arrival of Minerva Model Railways' GWR 'Iron Mink' box van and GWR 7ton gunpowder van, while Hatton's upscaled its 50ton bogie 'Warwell' well wagon for 'O' gauge with ten models issued covering GWR, LMS and LNER registered wagons through to modern Ministry of Defence (MOD) registered variants suitable for the 1970s-2000s era.

In mid-October Dapol filled another gap in the 'O' gauge market for BR-era modellers, with the arrival of its new 'O' gauge BR 20ton brake van, with certain examples proving very popular and selling out with the manufacturer almost instantly. Eight variants were offered in BR grey and BR bauxite with pre-TOPS and TOPS identities, together with a couple of unnumbered examples too.

Bumper crop

As in previous years it is a very difficult task to single out certain models from the impressive list that arrived this year. Hornby's all-new 'OO' gauge Stanier 'Duchess' 4-6-2 certainly impressed, as did Locomotion Models' GNR Stirling 'single' 4-2-2, which deservedly received the *Hornby Magazine* Model Railway Award for 'Best 'OO' gauge locomotive' at a ceremony at the Great Electric Train Show in October. However, the true stand-out 'OO' gauge model this year must be Rails of Sheffield's LNER Dynamometer Car, for its sheer level of detail with etched metal shields, ornate clerestory glazing, distinctive white measuring wheel, impressive interior detailing and novel lighting solution.

For 'N' gauge modellers, Bachmann's Class 40 received plaudits from readers who awarded it 'Best 'N' gauge locomotive' in the *Hornby Magazine* Model Railway Awards, but we should also applaud Revolution Trains who demonstrated just what can be achieved through 'people-power' with its crowd-funding of the stunning Class 390 Pendolino project. In 'O' gauge, both Dapol and Minerva Model Railways' GWR '57XX' 0-6-0PTs caught our eye... while the latter's digital sound-fitted GWR example also caught our ear! Dapol's new 'O' gauge BR 20ton brake vans are sure to prove popular at the rear of many a goods train in the coming weeks and months, while looking ahead, Heljan's 'O' gauge Class 25/3 Bo-Bo diesel was tantalisingly close to release as this issue of the *Hornby Magazine* Yearbook closed for press.

What a year – and there's more to come with plenty of outstanding projects yet to arrive. It's certainly going to be another exciting year ahead for modellers in all scales. ■

The Model Centre took delivery of its latest commission from Bachmann – the 22ton double bolster and plate wagons for 'OO' gauge.

'ATLANTIC' 4-4-2s

Before the advent of the racing 'Pacifics' of the 1930s another type of locomotive was breaking new ground in railway performance and achievement. The 'Atlantics' are not as well known as their later six-coupled cousins, but had an equally dramatic effect on British railway performance, as **EVAN GREEN-HUGHES** describes.

The London, Brighton and South Coast Railway based its 'Atlantic' designs on the Great Northern Railway 'C1' 4-4-2s. In 1933 Marsh 'H2' 4-4-2 2421 *South Foreland* approaches Lewes with an up train formed of Maunsell corridor stock and a Pullman dining car. O.J. Morris/Rail Archive Stephenson.

BRITISH 'ATLANTIC' STEAM LOCOMOTIVES (TENDER ONLY)				
DESIGNER	**RAILWAY**	**CLASS**	**INTRODUCED**	**LAST WITHDRAWN**
Ivatt	GNR	'C2'	1898	1945
Aspinall	LYR	Class 7	1899	1934
Ivatt	GNR	'C1'	1902	1950
Churchward	GWR	'Saint'	1903	1913 (rebuilt as 4-6-0)
Robinson	GCR	'C4'	1903	1950
Worsdell	NER	'C6'	1903	1948
Marsh	LBSCR	'H1'	1905	1951
Robinson	GCR	'C5'	1905	1947
Worsdell	NER	'C8'	1906	1935
Reid	NBR	'C11	1906	1939
Marsh	LBSCR	'H2'	1911	1958
Raven	NER	'C7'	1911	1948
Reid	NBR	'C10'	1911	1925
Gresley	LNER	'C9' (rebuilt 'C7')	1931	1943

North British Railway Reid 'H' (LNER 'C11') 'Atlantic' 509 *Duke of Rothesay* poses in photographic grey when new from North British Locomotives in 1921. Rail Archive Stephenson.

IN THE LATE 1800s THE STAPLE British express locomotive was the 4-4-0, a rugged and simple wheel arrangement, but one which presented constraints to the designer, particularly in respect of the length of boiler and also the design of the firebox, which had to be accommodated in the narrow space between the rear driving wheels. By extending the length of a locomotive and adding a pair of trailing wheels both these issues could be overcome. The resulting locomotives had a 4-4-2 wheel arrangement and were known as 'Atlantics'.

Pioneering work on 'Atlantics' was carried out by Henry Ivatt of the Great Northern Railway (GNR), whose 'C1' locomotive first appeared in 1898, and by John Aspinall of the Lancashire and Yorkshire Railway with his Class 7 'High Flyer' of 1899, following which the type was to rise to prominence and widespread use until superseded by 4-6-2 'Pacifics' some 20 years later.

Like many other types of locomotives the 'Atlantics' are said to have acquired their nickname from the USA where the 4-4-2 wheel arrangement was already in widespread passenger use by the mid 1890s. The Baldwin Locomotive Works had supplied the design to the Philadelphia and Reading's Atlantic line in 1894 and this may be where the name originated. However locomotive designers from all over the world were developing engines in similar ways and there were many examples of 'Atlantics' appearing in other countries at about the same time.

Although the design was to be at its most successful when applied to tender engines, in fact the first 4-4-2s in this country were tank locomotives. The Class 1 4-4-2T of the London, Tilbury and Southend Railway (LTS) appeared in 1880, starting a long relationship between this arrangement and the LTS which was to last for many decades. For this application the wheel arrangement was chosen because LTS locomotives had to be capable of running fast in both directions over a medium-length route, a design brief that required smaller wheels to guide at the front »

Gleaming in the sunlight at Nottingham Victoria in 1910, Ivatt's pioneer 'C2' class 'Atlantic' 990 *Henry Oakley* is being kept in fine condition by its crew. Freddy Gilford/Rail Archve Stephenson.

and rear and also frames capable of supporting adequate amounts of coal and water. This design was later developed for the London & South Western Railway (LSWR) while other locomotives with this wheel arrangement were constructed for the Great Northern (GNR), the Great Central (GCR), the Great Western (GWR), London & North Western (LNWR) and London, Brighton & South Coast (LBSCR) railways.

Tender development

Three of the UK's most prominent engineers were great personal friends and it cannot be a coincidence that all three began working up ideas for 'Atlantic' tender engines at around the same time. Henry Ivatt of the GNR was developing plans for his 'C1' at the same time as John Aspinall was working on the Class 7. Concurrently their colleague Wilson Worsdell of the North Eastern Railway (NER) was said to have considered an 'Atlantic' before settling on a 4-6-0 for work north of York.

Ivatt's engine came out of works about six months before Aspinall's in the form of 990 *Henry Oakley* which, although something of a prototype, immediately proved itself as powerful and fast. The key to its success was a large boiler which could supply seemingly endless amounts of steam and its wheel arrangement which ensured easy riding. As with most of the American engines, two outside cylinders were employed but these were found to be unduly small, at 18in x 24in, and restricted the work that the engine could do. Nevertheless the new 'Atlantic' proved to be so fast that Ivatt had to order his footplatemen not to drive it at its maximum performance due to the condition of some of the company's track!

Aspinall adopted a completely different approach to locomotive production and when the first of his Class 7s, 1400, appeared a few months after *Henry Oakley* it was considered to be a fully-worked-up production machine and was, in fact, the first of a batch of 20 which followed immediately afterwards. Known as 'High Flyers' because of their high-pitched boilers, they were radically different from the Great Northern's machines, particularly in that they were fitted with inside cylinders. The front end was very similar to the company's existing large-wheeled 4-4-0s, as was the front bogie, but the boiler was some 15ft long between the tube plates and was attached to a large Belpaire firebox.

The 'High Flyers' were certainly spectacular-looking machines with enormous splashers covering the 7ft 3in diameter driving wheels and, apart from some minor teething troubles, went straight into reliable service. Despite their huge appearance and power these engines were surprisingly light, weighing in at slightly less than some of the LNWR's existing 4-4-0s. They proved outstanding particularly when working the tightly-timed and competitive Liverpool to Manchester expresses and also over the company's core Pennine route between Manchester Victoria and York.

Back at the GNR, confidence in 990 was such that a further ten locomotives were constructed to the same basic design, but this time slightly larger cylinders were used. A four-cylinder version, 271, was added in 1902 but was not a great success and in due course was rebuilt to conform with the other engines. Larger boiler variations began to appear in 1902 and there were subsequent developments of the type with the addition of superheating and changes in cylinder size, as well as an attempt at a compound version. Nigel Gresley succeeded Ivatt in 1911 and no further 'Atlantics' were built, although more improvements were made to the existing engines for many years afterwards. In all forms these 'Atlantics' did superb work and enabled new levels of speed and train weights to become regular features of East Coast Main Line working.

In vogue

In 1903 it seemed as if the 'Atlantic' was going to become very much in fashion with locomotives of the wheel arrangement coming into service with the GCR, the NER and even the GWR.

The GCR's '8Bs' (later 'C4' under the London and North Eastern Railway) were part of an evaluation process to work out which would be the best design for working longer and heavier trains. Two examples were commissioned from Beyer, Peacock along with two very similar 4-6-0s and all four were based on the earlier 'B5' 4-6-0, having two outside cylinders, with the 'Atlantics' proving sufficiently successful that 25 more were added over subsequent years, these having bigger fireboxes than the prototype. These engines were known as 'Jersey Lillies', some say because they were so beautiful that they could be compared to contemporary music hall star Lilly Langtree, while others claim it was because the huge girth of their boiler was compared to that of an extremely large woman called Lilly who frequented one of the pubs near Gorton Works.

In the same year the 'C4s' appeared, Wilson Worsdell introduced his 'C6' to the NER. As his 'B13' and 'B14' 4-6-0s had proved rather unsuccessful he had to come up with something else and so he had taken himself off to the USA where he had been very impressed with the performance of the Pennsylvania Railroad's 4-4-2s. He would also by this time have seen his friend Ivatt's 'C1s' when they hauled trains into York. The result was an 'Atlantic' with a 200psi, 5ft 6in boiler with a very deep but narrow firebox and very large cylinders which had a tractive effort around 50% higher than the GNR's machines. The first, 532, left Gateshead works in November 1903 and was soon followed by ten more with the design being so successful that ten further examples were added in 1908, though with some differences. These related to the cylinders which were reduced in dimensions and to the main frames which were strengthened at the front. These locomotives were so successful that they were still hauling top link expresses on the East Coast Main Line north of York right up until the grouping of 1923. Withdrawals didn't begin until 1943 and two even managed to make it to nationalisation in 1948.

The Great Western's introduction to 'Atlantics' came about via a completely different route, which was probably unprecedented in British locomotive history. On his appointment as Chief Mechanical Engineer of that company in 1902 George Jackson Churchward was anxious to use the best of contemporary practice when drawing up the specifications for his new range of standard steam locomotives. As part of this process he ordered an 'Atlantic' locomotive from France based on the de Glehn compounds which were then doing extremely good work on the Nord Railway.

Delivered in October 1903 and named *La France* the locomotive was radically different from »

The Great Central Railway's Chief Mechanical Engineer John George Robinson developed the handsome '8B' (later 'C4' under the LNER) 4-4-2 class for its express services. '8B' 262 pilots 'Improved Director' 4-4-0 507 *Gerard Powys Dewhurst* at Guide Bridge as the pair prepares to depart with an up express in 1920. W.H. Whitworth/Rail Archive Stephenson.

The Great Western Railway experimented with the 4-4-2 wheel arrangement during development of the 'Saint' 4-6-0s with 13 of the class being built as 'Atlantics', though they were later rebuilt as 4-6-0s. In April 1906, 'Saint' 4-4-2 186 stands at Bristol Temple Meads before being named *Robin Hood* – it was rebuilt as a 4-6-0 in May 1912 and became 2986 *Robin Hood*. Robert Brookman/Rail Archive Stephenson

anything else that was operating in this country. Fitted with two low pressure cylinders between the frames and two high pressure ones outside, *La France* was clearly of foreign origin, despite its standard GWR tender, and was set to work against 4-4-0s of the 'City' and the 'Atbara' class as well as in comparison with 171 *Albion,* a 4-6-0 which had been modified to the 'Atlantic' wheel arrangement.

Although the trials provided Churchward with a lot of useful data he remained undecided as to the merits of the 'Atlantic' over the 4-6-0, and so 13 of his early 'Saint' class were constructed as 4-4-2s and six were built as 4-6-0s. Further work then convinced Churchward that the 4-6-0 had superior adhesive powers and so no further 'Atlantics' were built and, in time, those that had been were converted to the 4-6-0 wheel arrangement. It is perhaps interesting to note here that the Great Western had no need of the wide fireboxes necessary in other areas of the country, due to the high calorific value of the Welsh steam coal that the company used, which meant that less was required for producing steam at any given point.

With the 'Atlantic' being such a success on the East Coast route, it perhaps should have come as no surprise that when Douglas Earle Marsh

Aspinall LYR 'High Flyer' 4-4-2 1419 storms away from Poulton-le-Fylde with an express from Blackpool North in 1905. These engines had 7ft 3in driving wheels and inside cylinders. J.M. Tomlinson/Rail Archive Stephenson.

went to the LBSCR from the GNR in 1904 that he proposed that his new employers should consider use of the type for their principal expresses. Once approval had been obtained Marsh's course of action was, however, somewhat unusual in that he obtained a set of drawings from Doncaster of the latest engines and made only minimal alterations to them before sending them off to independent locomotive builder Kitson for construction to commence.

The result was the five members of the 'H1' class which were employed with much success on London to Brighton expresses and which were to last for almost half a century before being scrapped. Anyone looking at these engines could not miss their Doncaster pedigree, which was carried on to a second batch of six built in 1920, which were basically the same, although with some detail improvements.

Inspiring Scotland

By this time the success of the 'Atlantic' design was recognised far and wide and had come to the attention of the directors of the North British Railway (NBR) who were seeking to find new locomotives that would be masters of both the upper end of the East Coast Main Line and the steeply-graded 'Waverley Route'.

Logic would have argued that a 4-6-0 might have been more suitable for this type of work, but such was the popularity of the 'Atlantic' at this time that in November 1905 the company's board met and approved the construction of 14 heavy express locomotives, all of which were to be to the 4-4-2 wheel arrangement. Prepared to the design of William Paton Reid, the new engines had 6ft 9in driving wheels, two outside cylinders and a tractive effort of 21,170lbs, the second-highest of any 'Atlantic' built up to that time. Known as the 'H' but later 'C11' under the London and North Eastern Railway (LNER), the 14 engines were joined by a further six in 1911, with a final two following in 1920.

Unfortunately the North British 'Atlantics' had a somewhat chequered history. Initially their »

Ivatt 'C1' 4-4-2 3300 is about to take water from Langley troughs with the 4.30pm up Newcastle express for London King's Cross in 1930. Until the arrival of the first Gresley 'Pacifics' in the early 1920s, the 'Large Boilered' 4-4-2s were used for the Great Northern Railway's fastest passenger workings. Frank Hebron/Rail Archive Stephenson.

The Great Western Railway took a bold move of ordering three de Glehn compound 4-4-2s from France to evaluate the 'Atlantic' wheel arrangement. They were coupled to standard GWR tenders. The first of the three de Glehn compound 'Atlantics' 102 *La France* heads out of London Paddington past Royal Oak when new in 1904. Rail Archive Stephenson.

performance fell far short of what had been anticipated and there were reports of excessive coal consumption and oscillation, some of which reached board level. As a result comparative trials were organised with an LNWR 'Experiment' 4-6-0 but these proved inconclusive, with the results seeming to depend more on the skill of individual enginemen rather than the design of the engine itself. There was also opposition from the civil engineer who considered that the engines were too heavy for the track and structures. Nevertheless after a period of bedding in, the 'Atlantics' settled down to give a sterling performance and were to last well into the 1930s before being superseded by larger and more powerful designs.

Compounding

By 1905 designers were seeking ways of extracting even more power out of locomotives and one way that this could be done was by using compounding, which is a system by which both high and low pressure cylinders are provided in which steam is effectively used twice. Although popular on the continent and indeed fitted to the de Glehn locomotive that had been tried out on the GWR, the system had never been widely used in the UK. One of its exponents was the Great Central's John Robinson who had been impressed with work done by Walter Smith of the NER and this influenced him to place an order for two compound 'Atlantics' based on the 'C4'. The first of these appeared in December 1905 and were followed by two more in February 1906.

In these engines a central high pressure cylinder drove the leading axle and two more low pressure outside cylinders drove the rear axle and it was said that the design had a saving of around 2lbs of coal per mile, part of which was offset by the additional cost and complexity of the compound design. Later designated as the 'C5s', these engines were more successful than most compounds and were to last until the late 1940s.

The GNR also experimented with compound 'Atlantics' but these were an odd lot and it seems that the railway never came to any firm conclusion as to whether compounding was worth further investigation. The first was 292 which entered service in 1905, this was a four-cylinder machine which was superficially similar to the standard 'Atlantic' but which was fitted with four cylinders on the compound system. It lasted until 1928 and was then scrapped without development. The next locomotive, 1300, came about as a result of the GNR's board seeking designs for compounds from outside suppliers. The Vulcan Foundry offered an 'Atlantic' based on the French system and one was purchased but it soon acquired a formidable reputation for poor reliability and seemed to suffer from bad design. It was rebuilt as a simple engine in 1917 but scrapped soon afterwards. The final compound 'Atlantic' was 1421 which appeared in 1907. Again this was an Ivatt engine built at Doncaster and it followed closely the layout of 292, although with revised cylinder dimensions. It proved better in service than the previous effort, but no better than a standard engine, to which form it was converted in 1920.

A final attempt at compounding came from the NER which produced two four-cylinder engines, 730-731, with considerable input from Walter Smith, who was unfortunately to pass away before they were completed. In complete contrast to those of the GNR these were outstanding in traffic but were of little interest to the company's chief mechanical engineer Wilson Worsdell, whose designs they seemed to be belittling and in consequence no further development was carried out.

Developments at the NER therefore took a different route and in 1910 Vincent Raven, who

had succeeded Worsdell, produced the 'C7' three-cylinder 'Atlantic' which were to some extent the pinnacle of development of this type of engine. With their huge boilers, adequate cylinder size and 6ft 10in driving wheels these engines had a tractive effort of 19,300lbs and proved masters of all the work that was put before them, with 14 of the class just lasting until nationalisation.

Two of the 'C7s' were, however, selected for a most remarkable conversion by Nigel Gresley in 1931, emerging from Darlington works fitted with even bigger boilers and with a powered four-wheel 'booster' bogie of the American type replacing the rear pair of wheels. The idea was to provide some extra horsepower for the four and a half mile climb out of Edinburgh when heading south, most of which was at 1-in-95, and eliminate double heading.

Trials proved successful although the booster units were only of value at up to 25mph, which was about 5mph slower than the timetable required and there were difficulties in engaging it at speed. Results of the experiment were somewhat inconclusive and within five years the new Gresley 'Pacifics' were climbing out of Edinburgh at an average speed of 55mph, meaning that there was no reason to retain the equipment which was subsequently removed, the engines reverting to standard 'Atlantic' configuration for the rest of their lives.

As can be seen, the introduction of larger locomotives, in particular the 'Pacifics', rendered the 'Atlantic' design redundant within three decades of its introduction, yet the type had a profound influence over British railway locomotive development. Although it is now more than a century since the 'Atlantic' reigned supreme two former Great Northern engines have survived as part of the national collection, these being prototype 990 *Henry Oakley* and 251, the first of the large-boiler 'C1s'. Two replicas are also under construction. At the Bluebell construction of one of the 'H2s' is now advanced while at Didcot the Great Western Society is building a 4-6-0 'Saint' locomotive which will be capable, just like the prototype, of being run as an 'Atlantic' from time to time.

It is fitting that there has recently been a resurgence in interest in modelling locomotives of the 'Atlantic' type which for many years have lived under the shadow of their larger and more glamorous 'Pacific' descendants. Hopefully many more of these interesting locomotive classes will be available in future years. ■

North Eastern Railway 'C7' 4-4-2 2172 departs York with an express for Newcastle in 1933. The first of these large 4-4-2s were introduced in 1911 with the last being withdrawn in 1948. Gordon Hepburn/ Rail Archive Stephenson.

Forward to 2019

This year we have expanded our annual survey of future products to encompass carriages and wagons as well as sought after locomotives. With an impressive 150+ new products to look forward to across three scales, **MIKE WILD** looks ahead to 2019 and beyond and evaluates what our manufacturers will be delivering next.

Dapol has relaunched its project to produce the Bulleid 'Light Pacifics' for 'N' gauge in original and rebuilt forms. On July 2 1964 34078 *222 Squadron* makes a dramatic departure from Wadebridge. Dave Cobbe/ Railphotoprints.uk.

Hatton's 'O' gauge Gresley 'A3' 4-6-2 has reached the engineering sample stage offering a tantalising glimpse of the finished product.

THE PACE OF MODEL development shows no signs of slowing and in 2018 we saw new announcements on a regular basis alongside continuous delivery of those already promised. In this year's survey we have 87 locomotives – the highest number in two years – together with an impressive line-up of more than 60 new carriages and wagons in three scales.

With more than 150 models in total, including all carriage versions, this is our most comprehensive annual survey yet and brings together all the planned models announced up to mid-October when this Yearbook closed for press. As in previous years 'OO' gauge is leading the charge as Britain's most popular scale, but 'O' gauge is gaining ground again with an increasing and attractive range of products ranging from compact shunting and tank engines through to giant diesels for heavy main line freight. Rolling stock development is speeding up in 7mm scale too with Dapol being particularly proactive in this field.

2018 has also seen an increase in the number of retailers stepping up to commission their own products, and not just carriages and wagons. Hatton's Model Railways has proved its ability to deliver high quality ready-to-run products in 'OO' and 'O' gauge during the past 12 months and is currently working on more projects for both scales. Meanwhile Rails of Sheffield has commissioned two new steam locomotives for 'OO' gauge while The Model Centre has teamed up with Bachmann to produce a locomotive and wagon models for 'OO' too.

Keeping up with all this development is a challenge, but we are certain that there will be something to suit everyone in the accompanying tables whether you model Southern, Midland or Scottish railways, and in any period from the early 1900s through to the present day.

'OO' gauge

A number of significant locomotives have joined the listings in 2018, not least Hornby's plans for the Southern Region Maunsell 'Lord Nelson' 4-6-0, Stanier streamlined 'Princess Coronation' 4-6-2 and LNER 'J36' 0-6-0 – its first Scottish Region prototype. Seizing the opportunity to be part of the Scottish theme, Rails of Sheffield revealed that it was working with Bachmann to produce the Caledonian Railway '812' 0-6-0 at Model Rail Scotland in February 2018 and at the same event The Model Centre caught visitors' attention with its plans for the LNER 'G5' 0-4-4T.

Also joining the steam race in 'OO' was Dapol with its December announcements of the GWR 'Large Prairie' 2-6-2Ts and '63XX' 2-6-0s – and with a promise of simple sound installation and the latest generation Next18 decoder sockets.

For diesel and electric models Hatton's impressed with its announcement of a brand new Class 66 for 'OO' gauge – and with an extensive specification including sound compatibility, rotating axleboxes, myriad body and chassis variations and a bold list of 32 livery options. Sulzer Type 2s were also in focus with Bachmann stating that it would produce brand new versions of the Class 25/1 and restyled Class 25/2 while Heljan also chose to »

Oxford Rail released images of its 'OO' gauge 'N7' 0-6-2T in colour in mid-2018. Release is expected in the fourth quarter or 2018 or early 2019.

The BR Sulzer Type 2s are hot property in 2019 with Bachmann signing up to produce the Class 25/1 and 25/2 with Heljan working on the 25/3 variant for 'OO' gauge. Carrying BR blue Class 25/2 25136 runs through Chinley with a Peak Forest-Northwich ICI limestone train on September 5 1981. Railphotoprints.uk.

produce the final development of the versatile Bo-Bo, the Class 25/3, using its research for the 'O' gauge model as the basis.

New announcements for 2018 can't pass without mention of the Gas Turbine Model Project's proposed 'OO' gauge model of unique gas turbine prototype GT3. This locomotive used a steam locomotive style 4-6-0 chassis and mated it with a gas turbine power unit and was completed by English Electric in 1961. An official launch for the model was expected at the Warley National Model Railway Exhibition in November 2018.

Looking to the near future, several of this year's list are soon due to be in the shops for 'OO' gauge including Hornby's 'J36' and streamlined 'Coronation' – both due in December – while Hornby's 'Lord Nelson' is currently expected to arrive in January. Oxford Rail's LNER 'N7' 0-6-2T won't be far behind either – a great addition for Great Eastern section modellers – while Kernow Model Rail Centre's original North British built D600 series

Kernow Model Rail Centre continues development of its sought after 'OO' gauge D600 series 'Warship' models. Decorated samples are expected next.

'Warships' were entering the final phases of livery development during the autumn ahead of release. Bachmann's next 'OO' gauge locomotive was expected to be the Class 90 in March 2019 offering a second new choice of West Coast Main Line electric motive power after Hornby's Class 87 of 2018.

When it comes to rolling stock, wagons are clearly the priority of manufacturers at present while carriages take something of a back seat. Of the 20 vehicles listed 16 are goods wagons while we can also look forward to the release of Bachmann's highly anticipated 45ton Ransomes steam crane in 'OO' gauge too.

Accurascale is also making advances in developing its range of 'OO' gauge wagons following on from the success of its debut model - HUO 24.5ton hopper - with two cement wagons to suit different eras – both filling significant gaps in the market.

You can find the full list of locomotives in Table 1 with carriages and wagons in Table 2.

'N' gauge

The smaller of the three scales featured in our survey has been stable in 2018, but has begun to see a greater influx of crowd-funded models. Revolution Trains has been particularly successful in developing 'N' gauge models in this way with delivery of its Class 390 Pendolino and Class B four-wheel tanker in 2018.»

TABLE 1 - 'OO' GAUGE LOCOMOTIVES IN DEVELOPMENT

CLASS	REGION	MANUFACTURER	EXPECTED
GWR steam railmotor	Western	Kernow MRC	TBA
GWR 'Large Prairie' 2-6-2T	Western	Dapol	2019
GWR '63XX' 2-6-0	Western	Dapol	2019
GWR '94XX' 0-6-0PT	Western	Bachmann	2019
LBSCR 'Terrier' 0-6-0T	Southern	Rails of Sheffield/Dapol	2019
SR 'Lord Nelson' 4-6-0	Southern	Hornby	2019
Caledonian '812' 0-6-0	Scottish	Rails of Sheffield/Bachmann	TBA
Midland '1P' 0-4-4T	Midland	Bachmann	2019
LMS streamlined 'Coronation'	Midland	Hornby	2018
LNER 'G5' 0-4-4T	Eastern	TMC/Bachmann	TBA
LNER 'J36' 0-6-0	Scottish	Hornby	2018
LNER 'J70' 0-6-0VBT	Eastern	Bauer Media	TBA
LNER 'J72' 0-6-0T	Eastern	Bachmann	2019
LNER 'N7' 0-6-2T	Eastern	Oxford Rail	2018
LNER 'V2' 2-6-2	Eastern	Bachmann	2019
WD 'ROD' 2-8-0	Midland/Eastern	Bachmann	2019
Hudswell Clarke 0-6-0ST	Industrial	DJ Models	TBA
GT3 gas turbine 4-6-0	Midland	Gas Turbine Model Project	TBA
Class 20/3	Various	Bachmann	TBA
Class 21/29	Scottish	Dapol	TBA
Class 24/1	Various	Bachmann	2019
Class 25/1	Various	Bachmann	TBA
Class 25/2	Various	Bachmann	TBA
Class 25/3	Various	Heljan	2019
Class 41 'Warship'	Western	Kernow MRC	2018
Class 59	Western	Dapol	2019
Class 66	Various	Hatton's Model Railways	2019
Class 86/0	Midland/Scottish	Heljan	2019
Class 90	Various	Bachmann	2019
Class 92	Various	DJ Models	TBA
GWR AEC railcar	Western	Heljan	2020
Class 117	Various	Bachmann	2019
Class 121	Various	Bachmann	2019
Class 142	Midland/Eastern	Realtrack	2018
Class 158	Various	Bachmann	2019
Class 159	Southern	Bachmann	2019
Class 370 APT-P	Midland	Durham Trains/DJ Models	TBA
Class 410 4-BEP	Southern	Bachmann	TBA
Class 414 2-HAP	Southern	Bachmann	2019
Western Region six-car Pullman	Western	Bachmann	2019
L&B 2-6-2T ('OO9')	Southern	Heljan	2018
Quarry Hunslet 0-4-0ST ('OO9')	Industrial	Bachmann	TBA
Total: 42	**Steam:** 19	**Diesel/electric:** 23	

TABLE 2 - 'OO' GAUGE NEW CARRIAGES AND WAGONS IN DEVELOPMENT

VEHICLE	REGION	MANUFACTURER	EXPECTED
O&K JHA aggregate hopper	Western	Dapol	2019
Bogie Bolster E	Midland/Eastern	Dapol	2019
YCV 'Turbot' spoil wagon	Various	Dapol	2018
BR 24.5ton mineral wagon	Various	TMC/Bachmann	TBA
Cemflo cement tanker	Southern/Eastern	Accurascale	2019
PCA cement tanker	Various	Accurascale	2019
PGA four-wheel hopper	Various	Cavalex Models	2019
LNER 'Toad B' brake van	Eastern	Hornby	2018
LNER 'Toad E' brake van	Eastern	Hornby	2018
Rail Head Treatment Train	Various	Hatton's Model Railways	2019
FEA-E and FEA-S spine wagons	Various	Hatton's Model Railways	2019
45ton Ransomes steam crane	Various	Bachmann	2019
Bulleid 63ft corridor stock	Southern	Bachmann	TBA
BR Mk 1 POT van	Various	Bachmann	2018
VEA four-wheel van	Various	Bachmann	TBA
Prestwin twin silo cement wagon	Various	Bachmann	TBA
LMS 'Parrot' bogie wagon	Midland	Bachmann	2019
BR 'Warflat' bogie wagon	Various	Bachmann	2019
Ashover Light Railway carriage	Narrow gauge	Bachmann	TBA
Four-wheel slate wagons	Narrow gauge	Bachmann	2019
'Boche Buster' rail gun	Southern	Oxford Rail	2019
IZA Cargowaggon twins	Various	Kernow Model Rail Centre	2019
PRA china clay wagon	Western	Kernow Model Rail Centre	2019
LSWR road van	Southern	Kernow Model Rail Centre	TBA
BOC liquid nitrogen tanker	Various	Olivias Trains/Heljan	2019

Hornby's all-new streamlined 'Princess Coronation' was scheduled to arrive during December for 'OO' gauge. This is the latest engineering sample.

At the International N Gauge Show Revolution revealed a list of new project proposals including the Class 128 Diesel Parcels Railcar, IPA car carriers and Cemflo cement tankers in conjunction with Accurascale. The same show saw the launch of a new manufacturer in Sonic Models with a ready-to-run model of the VEA four-wheel van.

Elsewhere DJ Models has moved its focus onto the GWR 'King' 4-6-0 for 'N' gauge, again with crowd-funding support, while Durham Trains of Stanley has been promoting an 'N' gauge model of the APT-P through the same funding route (as well as a 'OO' gauge version) produced by DJ Models.

Bachmann's Graham Farish range is close to releasing its South

TABLE 3 - 'N' GAUGE NEW LOCOMOTIVES IN DEVELOPMENT

CLASS	REGION	MANUFACTURER	EXPECTED
GWR 'King' 4-6-0	Western	DJ Models	TBA
SR 'C' 0-6-0	Southern	Bachmann	2019
SR 'West Country' 4-6-2	Southern	Dapol	TBA
SR rebuilt 'West Country' 4-6-2	Southern	Dapol	TBA
LMS '8F' 2-8-0	Midland	Bachmann	TBA
LNER 'J72' 0-6-0T	Eastern	Bachmann	TBA
Hunslet 'J94' 0-6-0ST	Eastern	DJ Models	TBA
Hudswell Clarke 0-6-0ST	Industrial	DJ Models	TBA
Hunslet 0-6-0DM	Industrial	N Gauge Society	2018
Class 17	Eastern/Scottish	DJ Models	On hold
Class 23	Eastern	DJ Models	TBA
Class 31 (refurbished)	Various	Bachmann	2018
Class 41 prototype HST	Western/Midland	Dapol	2019
Class 50	Midland/Western	Dapol	2018
Class 59	Western	Dapol	TBA
Class 92	Various	DJ Models	TBA
Class 92	Various	Revolution Trains	2018
Class 128	Western/Midland	Revolution Trains	Proposed
Class 142	Midland/Eastern	Dapol	2019
Class 158	Various	Graham Farish	TBA
Class 319	Midland/Southern	Bachmann	TBA
Class 321	Midland/Eastern	Revolution Trains	TBA
Class 370 APT-E	Midland	Durham Trains/DJ Models	Proposed
APT-E	Midland	Revolution Trains	Proposed
Total: 24	**Steam:** 9	**Diesel/electric:** 15	

Hornby's LNER 'Toad' brake vans were due imminently for 'OO' gauge as this Yearbook closed for press in October.

Heljan is making the Class 25/3 for 'OO' gauge using the research generated for its 'O' gauge model of the same design.

Hornby's LNER 'J36' 0-6-0 is expected to be its next locomotive arrival in December 2018.

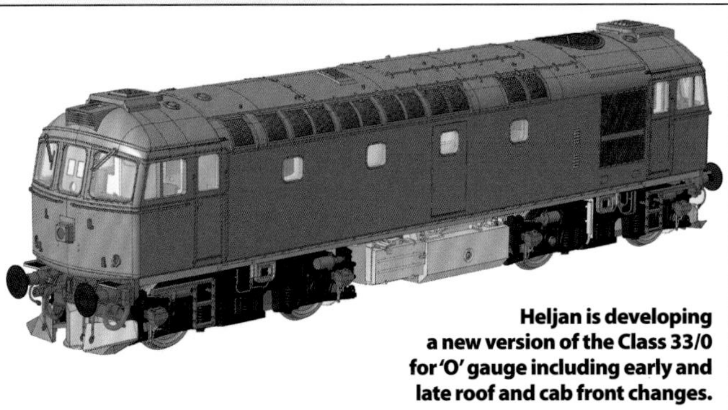

Heljan is developing a new version of the Class 33/0 for 'O' gauge including early and late roof and cab front changes.

Hatton's all-new 'OO' gauge Class 66 is making strides towards production.

The long requested Class 56 for 'O' gauge is to be delivered by Heljan following its announcement of plans for the model at the Telford Gauge O Guild exhibition in September 2018. Here construction sector Class 56 56033 passes the site of Box station at the head of 4C13 - the 11.11am Calvert-Bath/Bristol waste train empties on April 30 1993. John Chalcraft/Railphotoprints.uk.

TABLE 4 - 'N' GAUGE NEW CARRIAGES AND WAGONS IN DEVELOPMENT

VEHICLE	REGION	MANUFACTURER	EXPECTED
VEA four-wheel van	Various	Sonic Models	2019
KFA container flat	Various	Revolution Trains	2019
Sturgeon spoil wagon	Various	Revolution Trains	TBA
HOA aggregate hopper	Various	Revolution Trains	TBA
IPA car carrier	Various	Revolution Trains	TBA
SECR 'Birdcage' carriages	Southern	Graham Farish	2019
LNER Thompson corridor stock	Eastern	Graham Farish	TBA
BR Mk 2F carriages	Various	Graham Farish	TBA
BR Mk 2 DBSO	Eastern/Scottish	Graham Farish	TBA
TEA 100ton tanker	Various	Graham Farish	2019
Midland 20ton brake van	Midland	Graham Farish	2019
HIA aggregate hopper	Various	Dapol	TBA
BR Mk 3 sleeping car	Various	Dapol	2019
Prototype HST Mk 3 carriages	Western/Eastern	Dapol	2019
PCA cement hopper	Various	Realtrack Models	2019
PGA aggregate hopper	Various	Cavalex Models	TBA
Cemflo cement tanker	Southern/Eastern	Revolution/Accurascale	2019
Shark ballast plough	Various	DJ Models	2019
HUO 24.5ton hopper	Midland/Eastern	DJ Models	TBA

Eastern and Chatham Railway 'C' 0-6-0 and the same railway company's 'Birdcage' carriages while Dapol has been making great strides in development of its relaunched Class 50 for the scale.

Dapol has also recently revitalised its plans to develop the Bulleid 'West Country'/'Battle of Britain' 4-6-2s in original and rebuilt forms. It was relaunched during its annual open day in October 2018 – a project which many are looking forward to seeing brought to completion.

As in 'OO' gauge, wagons dominate the rolling stock category in 'N' gauge ranging from modern bogie stone hoppers to container flats, cement wagons and a Midland 20ton brake van.

See Table 3 and 4 for the full listings. »

Bachmann's next big locomotive arrival for 'OO' will be the Class 90 overhead electrics. They are due in March 2019.

As well as the Class 117 three-car DMU, Bachmann has been continuing development of its 'OO' gauge Class 121 single-car DMUs.

'O' gauge

Development of new products for 'O' gauge has continued to gather pace with Dapol being one of the most proactive manufacturers for the scale. During the past year it has added three locomotives, two Diesel Multiple Units (DMUs), Mk 1 carriages and six new wagons to its plans for the future. Four of the wagons are to be manufactured at Dapol's own factory in Chirk.

Heljan has had a busy year too and alongside delivery of its Class 20, 25/3, 128 and GWR 'Prairie' it has also announced plans for the Class 56 in 'O' gauge alongside a brand new version of the Class 33/0 covering early and late variations and the GWR AEC railcar. It is also continuing work on its Class 117, 121 and 122 DMUs – including the Class 149 and Class 150 trailer cars for the Class 121 and 122 respectively. It has also confirmed that the previously announced Class 120 has been put on hold for the time being due to a lack of drawings and information.

DMUs have proved to be a popular subject as Dapol is also producing ready-to-run 'O' gauge Class 121 and 122 railcars – both of which are expected to arrive either in late 2018 or early 2019.

Rolling stock is a busy category in 'O' gauge too with Dapol leading the way with goods wagons while its Mk 1 carriages look set to be popular releases too. Accurascale has also made its first move into 'O' gauge with the announcement of the HUO 24.5ton hopper for the scale. Meanwhile Hatton's is continuing development of its Gresley corridor stock for 'O' alongside its models of the Gresley's 'A3' and 'A4' class 'Pacifics' for release in 2019.

Tables 5 and 6 detail the full list of ready-to-run mass-produced 'O' gauge locomotives, carriages and wagons currently planned.

Overview

The choice of forthcoming ready-to-run rolling stock is mind-boggling with so many products in development across many eras, regions and now four gauges too with the advent of 'OO9'. In fact there is something to suit nearly every layout situation from industrial sidings to branch lines and main lines and in any scale.

The continued support for ready-to-run 'O' gauge is fascinating to watch while Bachmann is also developing more products for 'OO9' narrow gauge following the successful arrival of its Baldwin 4-6-0T in mid-2018.

For the greatest variety 'OO' gauge is still king of the gauges and you can be sure that with each project our manufacturers will be pushing the boundaries of detail and operational value. We're looking forward to seeing each and every one of these new models cross our desk and giving you the full story on the finished product. ■

The Class 121 and 122 DMUs are being delivered in 'O' gauge by Dapol. The first are expected to arrive before the end of 2018.

'N' gauge Southern modellers will soon have the chance to own a SECR 'C' 0-6-0 through Graham Farish.

Above: Dapol continues to push forward with new rolling stock projects in 'O' gauge. Its latest announcements are the YCV 'Turbot' spoil wagon together with its predecessor the Bogie Bolster E.

THE HEADLINES

PLANNED 'OO' GAUGE NEW LOCOMOTIVES

	2015	2016	2017	2018	2019
Steam:	26	25	21	15	19
Diesel:	18	20	25	23	23
Total:	44	45	46	38	42

PLANNED 'N' GAUGE NEW LOCOMOTIVES

	2015	2016	2017	2018	2019
Steam:	17	13	9	10	9
Diesel:	11	12	14	16	15
Total:	28	25	23	26	24

PLANNED 'O' GAUGE NEW LOCOMOTIVES

	2015	2016	2017	2018	2019
Steam:	3	3	9	8	7
Diesel:	9	7	11	11	14
Total:	12	10	20	18	21
Overall total:	**84**	**80**	**89**	**82**	**87**

Oxford Rail has received decorated samples of its 'OO' gauge 'Boche Buster' rail gun.

The latest samples to be received by Hatton's are decorated versions of its Rail Head Treatment Train wagons for 'OO' gauge.

TABLE 5 - 'O' GAUGE NEW LOCOMOTIVES IN DEVELOPMENT			
CLASS	REGION	MANUFACTURER	EXPECTED
GWR '14XX' 0-4-2T	Western	Dapol	2019
GWR '43XX' 2-6-0	Western	Heljan	2018
GWR '45XX' 2-6-2T	Western	Lionheart Trains/Dapol	2019
LNER 'A3' 4-6-2	Eastern	Hatton's/Heljan	2019
LNER 'A4' 4-6-2	Eastern	Hatton's/Heljan	2019
LNER 'Y1'/'Y3' 4wVBT	Eastern	Dapol	2019
Manning Wardle 'K' 0-6-0ST	Industrial	Minerva Model Railways	2019
Ruston 48DS	Various	Little Loco Co	2019
Class 03	Various	Heljan	2019
Class 22	Western	Little Loco Co	2019
Class 33/0	Southern	Heljan	2019
Class 47	Various	Heljan	2019
Class 50 (refurbished)	Midland/Western	Heljan	2018
Class 56	Midland/Eastern	Heljan	TBA
Class 117	Western/Midland	Heljan	2019
Class 120	Western	Heljan	On hold
Class 121/149	Western/Midland	Heljan	2019
Class 121	Western/Midland	Dapol	2019
Class 122/150	Western/Midland	Heljan	2019
Class 122	Western/Midland	Dapol	2019
GWR AEC railcar	Western	Heljan	TBA
Total: 21	**Steam:** 7	**Diesel:** 14	

TABLE 6 - 'O' GAUGE NEW CARRIAGES AND WAGONS IN DEVELOPMENT			
VEHICLE	REGION	MANUFACTURER	EXPECTED
Bogie Bolster E	Midland/Eastern	Dapol	2019
YCV 'Turbot' spoil wagon	Various	Dapol	2019
HEA four-wheel hopper	Various	Dapol	2019
VEA four-wheel van	Various	Dapol	2019
BR 24.5ton HUO hopper	Midland/Eastern	Accurascale	2019
BR Mk 1 BSK	All	Dapol	2019
BR Mk 1 SK	All	Dapol	2019
BR Mk 1 CK	All	Dapol	2019
BR Mk 1 SO	All	Dapol	2019
LNER Gresley Open Third	Eastern	Hatton's Model Railways	2019
LNER Gresley Corridor Third	Eastern	Hatton's Model Railways	2019
LNER Gresley Brake Composite	Eastern	Hatton's Model Railways	2019
9ft wheelbase five-plank open	All	Dapol	2019
9ft wheelbase seven-plank open	All	Dapol	2019
9ft wheelbase salt wagon	Various	Dapol	2019
9ft wheelbase lime wagon	Various	Dapol	2019
BR Mk 1 non-corridor Brake	Various	Darstaed	2019
BR Mk 1 non-corridor Lavatory second	Various	Darstaed	2019
BR Mk 1 non-corridor Composite	Various	Darstaed	2019
BR Mk 1 non-corridor Second Open	Various	Darstaed	2019
BR Mk 1 non-corridor Second	Various	Darstaed	2019

Dapol is aiming to impress 'OO' gauge Western Region modellers with brand new versions of the GWR 'Large Prairie' 2-6-2T and '63XX' 2-6-0. On May 23 1963 'Mogul' 6394 approaches Cemmes Road with a long mixed goods. Dave Cobbe Collection/ Railphotoprints.uk.